MAKING OF LONDON

BY

SIR LAURENCE GOMME, F.S.A.

AUTHOR OF 'PRINCIPLES OF LOCAL GOVERNMENT'
'THE GOVERNANCE OF LONDON,' ETC.

OXFORD
AT THE CLARENDON PRESS
1912

HENRY FROWDE M.A.

PUBLISHER TO THE UNIVERSITY OF OXFORD

LONDON, EDINBURGH, NEW YORK

TORONTO AND MELBOURNE

PREFACE

THIS book does not attempt to present an argument for the particular view of the history of London which it conveys. It merely states the case for that view. A statement is necessary because until it is clear what can be said to arise from the complicated network of record, archaeology, tradition, and contemporary history, nothing can be done to test the conclusions and compare them with what other historians have written.

London possesses greater wealth not only in traditions and records, but also in archaeological discoveries, than any other city in Great Britain. This fact alone pronounces for its greatness. Its greatness tells for a unique position among local institutions, and it is this position which demands investigation from every side.

The value of tradition and custom as elements of history is persistently ignored when the institutions or early conditions of our own country are concerned. They are admitted as valuable aids in the understanding of the history of ancient Rome or ancient Athens, of any of the Italic or Greek cities or centres of civilization. I claim the same value for them in the history of London. They exist, and their existence means something. My interpretation of their meaning is guided by historical or archaeological facts, and I claim that this interpretation should have a hearing.

I have not attempted a popular history, but have aimed at giving a fairly complete survey of the total

facts which lead up to the full history. In a sense
I attempted to give a full history in my larger work,
The Governance of London published in 1908. But
the subject grows upon one, and I hope to extend the
evidence collected in that work and bring out in
a second edition the extensions and corrections which
are needed. In the meantime it is well to supply the
student with a succinct account of the general line
of argument to which I am working forward, for it
will help him to realize the new point of view, and
perhaps to win him from the great influence which the
distinguished name of E. A. Freeman has exercised in
the opposite direction.

There is a further purpose which I hope this book
will serve, and that is the stimulus it may give to
the study of local history, not only by those who are
still at work in their schools, but by those who take an
intelligent interest in the great city of which they are
citizens. London loses much by its magnitude. It is
all to the good when researches into its history bring
out the continuous historical association of greater
London with the smaller London, and of all the
Londons with the historic city which they surround.
One is apt to lose sight of this. But there is no fact
more clearly to be adduced from the history of London,
there is no fact of greater significance ; and the extraordinary circumstance which thus brings together
history and modern conditions should never be lost
sight of. Every Londoner should know that the city
was an independent institutional unit while the area
outside its walls was being settled by the early English
conquerors of the country, that it remained with much
of its independence untouched during Anglo-Saxon

times, that it fought constitutionally for that independence during the great period of Plantagenet rule, and that at last, under Tudor rule and all the after influences of Tudor rule, it took its place among English cities and did its full share of national duty during all the great crises which have befallen the country All this it is necessary to know in order to be inspired by the greatness and the necessities of modern London. Statesman, citizen, and school-child all need to know the story of the making of London, and so far as this book conduces to this end it will have served its purpose.

I have to a limited extent used passages in former writings of my own, but these are not numerous and they are only adopted where it has been necessary to travel over precisely the same ground as I have before attempted. I am greatly indebted to Mr. Emery Walker, who has spared no pains in procuring illustrations for the book; most of them are from his photographs.

LAURENCE GOMME.

The Mound, Long Crendon, Bucks.
    December, 1911

The Houses of Parliament, from the River.

CONTENTS

LIST OF ILLUSTRATIONS

CHAPTER I

THE EVOLUTION OF THE SITE

The river Thames has made London. It was along its waters that the first people who settled on the spot which was to be known as London floated to their destiny; or it was along its banks that they crept slowly and painfully. It was under the shelter of one of its tributaries, the Fleet, that new-comers, who were probably Celts, settled and built their earliest dwellings, and then finally their stockaded stronghold It was the great river which made the Lundinium of the Romans. It was the protection afforded by the river which awakened the Anglo-Saxons to the importance of London, and made it onward from Alfred's time the political centre. It was the Thames which saved London from being conquered by the Norman, and which allowed the Norman coming to it friendliwise to develop its strength so greatly. All through the ages it is the river which is the central part of London's life, and when James the First threatened to remove the capital from London the unanswerable reply of the Lord Mayor, 'But your Majesty cannot remove the Thames,' strikes the key-note for all periods.

This great river is part of continental geology. The depression of the Thames valley represents and is physically a continuation of that which extends from

Valenciennes, by Douai, Bethune, Therouanne, and thence to Calais.   Britain in the earliest days of its occupation by man was physically part of the conti- nent, and some six hundred feet above its present level, the present coastal seas being then a great tract of low, undulating land, while the rivers of our eastern coast, the Thames, Medway, Humber, and Tyne, joined the Rhine, the Weser, and the Elbe to form a river flowing through the valley of the German Ocean.[1]

Perhaps what this great geological fact meant may best be indicated by the discoveries made in 1882 during the deep excavation at Charing Cross for the building of Messrs. Drummond's Bank.   There were dug out from the clay foundations over a hun- dred fossils, and the catalogue of the principal items is thus given   'Bones of the cave lion (*Felis leo*); tusks and bones of the mammoth, tusks and bones of extinct elephants (*Elephas primigenius, Elephas antiquus*); remains of extinct Irish deer (*Cervus me- gaceros*), remains of red deer; remains of a species allied to the fallow deer (*Cervus browni*), remains of rhinoceros; remains of extinct oxen (*Bos primigenius*) —from the pleistocene gravels   Bones of the horse, the sheep, and the shorthorn (Celtic) (*longifrons*)—from recent deposits.'   This is one of the most important finds of this nature, and the most recent find was in 1909, when remains of the mammoth and woolly rhinoceros occurred at various points between the Chingford branch of the Great Eastern Railway and Roding Road, Homerton, at a depth of nearly twenty- five feet in the gravel deposits of the river Lea.

[1] Whitaker, *Geology of London*, 12, Boyd Dawkins, *Early Man in Britain*, 1 1

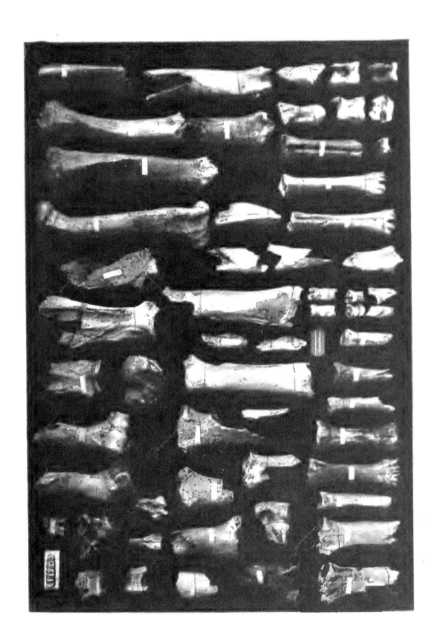

What the site of the future London actually was in this earliest of times we cannot even conjecture. We know that the palaeolithic savage who fought his way against fellow savage and against animals—fought his way to a simple home under the trees of pathless forests or on the open banks of the river or lake which finally became our Thames—did nothing of a constructive character to assist nature in making the homes of man here. He did not even make a solid house. He used the forest trees for his home ; he found the flints which he fashioned for his weapons of defence and attack, or for his implements of toil, on the surface or immediately under the surface of the ground : he hunted the animals and caught the fish for his principal food. and used the wild fruits to supplement these.

The surface which was trodden and occupied in this way by the palaeolithic men of this part of continental Britain was not our surface. Six hundred feet higher than our surface, it is now twenty feet beneath our surface. The palaeolithic land of Britain has not only sunk, but has had imposed on it fresh strata. This is shown by the discoveries of geologists, who have come across the stone implements of the palaeolithic savage at a depth of twelve to twenty feet below the present surface.

It happens that the 'palaeolithic floor', as it has been called. is one of the conspicuous features of the strata of London. Mr. Worthington Smith [1] has traced its extent and depth from various excavations which have yielded implements. The discoveries show this floor to have been on the top of the river gravel, and

_____

[1] *Man the Primeval Savage*, cap. xv.

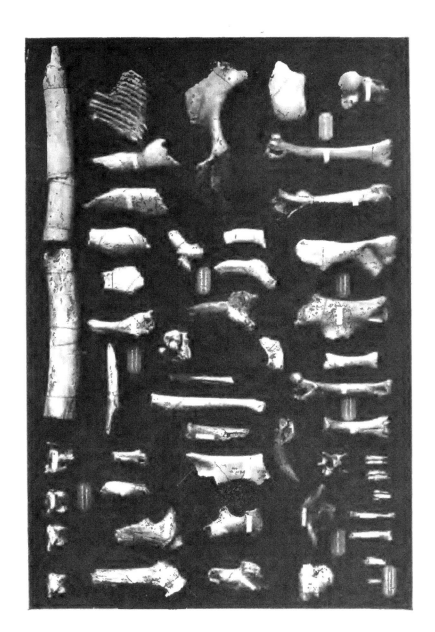

to include Stamford Hill and Tottenham on the north, and Higham Hill, Walthamstow, Woodford, Snaresbrook, Wanstead, and Barkingside on the east, coming into London at Hackney, Stoke Newington Common, Clapton, Kingsland, Dalston, London Fields, Clerkenwell, Drury Lane, Gray's Inn Lane, and the City, at all of which points implements have been found [1]

Between the palaeolithic age, which is now discoverable from remains beneath the site of modern London, and the neolithic age, which is the next discoverable occupation era, there is no certain connecting link. Britain was submerged by a great ice wave, and some authorities think that when this disappeared before the advancing warmer climate there could have been no living representatives of man in Britain. If this is so, neolithic man came to the site of London without getting into conflict or even into contact with his palaeolithic precursor The land was gradually sinking, and the subsidence, which is proved by the submerged forests beneath the Bristol Channel and the sea at Land's End, was going on throughout the neolithic age, ceasing somewhere about three thousand years ago.[2] The present natural surface of the site of London was formed then, and from this age we have practically continuous history.

It is not probable that neolithic man did much to alter the site of later London. They buried their chiefs, at all events, in burrows or rude stone sepulchres of the dolmen type. They often lived in caves in the neighbourhood of quarries, from which they gathered the

[1] *Anthropological Institute,* viii. 275-9.
[2] Holmes, *Ancient Britain,* 61.

BARROWS ON THE WILTSHIRE DOWNS.

flint to make their weapons and implements, specimens
of which have been found in London.   They undoubtedly constructed strongholds for defence, as many
examples in Britain prove, and it may be that the
stronghold which existed on the height where St. Paul's
now stands was constructed and first occupied by neolithic man.   But a stronghold with its surrounding
barrows do not materially alter the face of nature, as
one can see for oneself in Wiltshire or Dorsetshire,
where the evidence for neolithic man is so strongly
persistent

The first people who were builders as well as settlers,
homelanders as well as conquerors, were undoubtedly
the Celts.   Probably they were a bronze-using people
when they first arrived on these shores   At the junc-
ture of the Fleet river with the Thames they settled
in a fashion in which no predecessor of theirs had
settled.   Their settlement had a name, London, and
this alone constitutes a difference in its character
which is of great significance.   Their first business was
to construct residences, protected from human enemies
as from animals, adequately provided with the necessary water supply, and near enough to natural food
grounds for their hunters and fishermen to procure
what they needed, and to upland soil and downs upon
which their women and slaves would cultivate their
cereal foods.   Their second act was to create a stronghold
to which they might retreat with their cattle and their
grain when attacked by enemies.   Their enemies were
numerous.   Men of the same blood but not of the
same tribal unit were their enemies, and the men of
London had to take care that the men of Verulam, the
men of Croydon and those who occupied the Surrey

downs did not join perhaps with the displaced neolithic folk and successfully drive them forth from their
splendid settlement on the Thames.

It is at this point of history that the hand of man
begins its prominent part in fashioning the site of
London   The two preceding epochs left the heights
and the stretch of wide waters on their way to the sea
almost as nature willed.   The third epoch differs from
these.   The busy brains and hands of man having
begun to operate, we have changes to reckon with
which must direct our conception of the story to be
unfolded into totally different channels.   The making
of London began by inroads upon the natural site.
It has continued until we have lost views of the natural
site altogether.   The first work began on the river.
Underneath the bed of the Fleet river, now covered
over with pavements and bridges and houses, and along
the low-lying morass now occupied by Finsbury, have
been found the structural remnants of the Celtic habitations of London   First General Pitt-Rivers, and
subsequently Mr. F. W. Reader, have conducted in-
vestigations, which undoubtedly prove the existence
of lake habitations on these sites.   The value of this
discovery is not limited to the material objects.   If
there were lake habitations on the banks of the Fleet
river in London, there were lake-habitation culture
and social organization, and these were of a definite
and important character.

The tribes who lived on the banks of the Fleet river
in pile-dwellings were on a surface several feet below
the modern level of Fleet Street.   The banks of the
Fleet were steep, as we may know from the position of
'Break-neck Steps' a narrow court and ascent leading

from Fleet Street to the Old Bailey—it is no longer in existence—which was undoubtedly formed out of the steep banks of the river. Alongside these banks, about 70 to 80 yards from the site of the later wall, great timber piles were driven, with cross-logs joining them to the shore, and on the wooden platform thus constructed were built extensive wooden buildings, the homes at ordinary times of the tribesmen. There, over the waters of the Fleet river, or over the shallow waters of the lagoon which then occupied the site of modern Finsbury, the earliest Londoners lived their primitive life. They were protected in their homes from the assaults of wild animals, and to an extent from the sudden assault of enemies belonging to other tribes. Gradually, how gradually it is impossible to say, they enlarged their sphere of action. Their success against enemies probably brought them fresh combinations of enemies, and it became necessary to add to their means of defence. This they accomplished by constructing on the height above what is now Ludgate Hill, where St. Paul's stands, a stronghold, with earthen ramparts towards the land side and washed on three sides by the waters of the Thames and its tributaries, or the lagoons which its tributaries were slowly draining. A stronghold such as this was can well be depicted from others which have not been obliterated by the growth of a city. It was the place of defence. It stood out from the morass and forest which surrounded it; it was defended by two or three valla with deep fosses between them, and it was definitely constructed for defence. 'The steep ascent of Ludgate Hill', says Mr. Loftie, 'is formed of a clay-bank originally rising like a cliff forty feet above the river, and this was one

THE FLEET RIVER IN THE NINETEENTH CENTURY.

(From an etching by J. W. Archer, published in 1841.)

of the sides of the stronghold '.[1]   No doubt it stood many an assault ; no doubt too it withstood those assaults successfully.   It was an ideal site and an ideal position.

It is just such a site and position that Julius Caesar describes in his commentary on the expedition into Britain.   'He learned from the envoys', he says. 'that the stronghold of Cassivellaunus. which was protected by woods and marshes, was not far off, and that a considerable number of men and of cattle had assembled in it.   The Britons apply the name of stronghold [*oppidum*] to any woodland spot difficult of access and fortified with a rampart and trench, to which they are in the habit of resorting in order to escape a hostile raid.'   All these facts fit the then conditions of London, and one great authority, General Pitt-Rivers, proclaims his belief that the stronghold of Cassivellaunus was indeed London.[2]

We cannot decide this   It is beyond the ken of history   But there are important facts in its favour.

First and most important of all, there is the configuration of ancient London.   Few people probably grasp the fact that parts of modern London are below high-water mark and that the centre of London is overlooked by hills on the north and south. The valley of the Thames was in these early days represented by the river-bed in its present course and by lagoons of shallow waters spreading from its banks. Between the Ravensbourne and the Wandle there is a vast district, represented by modern Rotherhithe, Bermondsey, Newington, Southwark, North Lambeth,

[1] *Hist of London,* 1 20.

[2] *Anthropological Review* (1867), vol. v. p lxxviii.

and North Battersea, which was covered by the lagoon
waters and is even now several feet below high-water
mark. The north is higher ground, but Brompton,
Pimlico, and Chelsea represent the ancient lagoon
waters of the Thames. Rising from this wide-spread-
ing lagoon the lands stretched up to the heights north
and south of the Thames, 365 feet at the Crystal
Palace and 440 at Highgate. Opposite the widest part
of the lagoon on the south, and close up to the bed of
the Thames as it is now, there rises on the north a
height which comes close down to the water's edge.
It is a commanding situation. It is the first defensive
position of the Thames and it commands the route
northwards. This height, if defended, would threaten
the march of an invader northwards, and it is here
that we find placed the stronghold of Lyndun, the
stronghold of the waters. The march of Cassivellaunus
from Kent was along the British trackway, later to
be known as Watling Street, which led to London,
and, with this fact in mind, Mr. Conybeare believes
London was the objective of this great march. The
British chieftain would have gained his first defensive
point in opposing the Roman army.

Secondly, the conquerors of the Britons built a camp
here very soon after they had completed the first stages
of their conquest, and this camp grew quickly into
a great meeting-place for Roman commerce. This is
what might have been expected by what we know
of Roman practices elsewhere in Britain. They utilized
the great defensive places of the native population
whom they conquered.

And, finally, London has only one competitor for the
stronghold of the British chieftain, namely, Verulam,

which also may have been a British stronghold before
it became a Roman camp. Not only, however, is there
no direct evidence of a British *oppidum* at Verulam,[1]
but there is a curious break in the history of British
Verulam, as revealed by the numismatic remains, which
does not tell in its favour.[2]   On the other hand, right
at the beginning of history there is a point which
does not touch Verulam but which tells in favour of
London.   Caesar is describing the passage of the
Thames just before he branches off into his general description of the British strongholds, and one may read
into the narrative that this difficult crossing, causing
a pause in his great march into the interior of Britain,
had caused also a corresponding pause in his narrative.
Nothing is more certain about the splendid artistry of
Caesar's famous book than that it is based upon his actual
experiences.   Action and thought go together.   His
narrative moves forward or halts just where his military operations move forward or halt.   And his halt at
the passage of the Thames is reflected in the pause in
his narrative.   At this pause he describes what he
learns about the stronghold of Cassivellaunus   The
passage of the Thames had brought the point to his
mind, and thus, when we are trying to penetrate the
obscurity of history, the Thames leads us to London.

If, therefore, history does not exactly decide the
question, there is enough evidence in its favour for

[1] Mr McClure makes a point in favour of Verulam being an ancient
British site in his derivation of the name from a misunderstood root
name, 'Werlam,' which became 'Waetling' in English, the stronghold
taking its name from the British trackway which had become known
as 'Waetling Street'.   See his *British Place Names in their historical
setting*, 39–41.

[2] Evans, *Anc. British Coins*, 226

us provisionally to adopt the idea that the stronghold of London was the tribal stronghold of Cassivellaunus, the British chieftain who withstood the great Roman. One could wish for no better beginning for London. It is true that this beginning had a sudden and almost complete ending, which will presently be described, but even so London thus becomes one of those great strongholds of the world the conquest of which has led to the turning of history into new channels. Even Caesar could not afford to neglect it. He had to conquer it or himself be conquered. He chose the bolder course, and thus ended the first chapter in the making of London.

CHAPTER II

EARLIEST RELICS OF MAN IN LONDON

It will have been gathered from the previous chapter that palaeolithic man roaming over the unnamed site twenty feet beneath modern London, neolithic man using the site more definitely and perhaps beginning the fashioning of the later London, and the Celtic Britons settling in London, constructing there a stronghold for their defence and giving to it definite name and history, have not left many relics of their existence. Such relics as exist, however, are worth consideration, even if only for the confirmation they give to what is discoverable from the other sources which we have examined.

The palaeolithic implements of London are some of the most famous of their class and 'the Thames valley', says Sir John Evans, 'may lay claim to the first recorded discovery of any flint implement in the Quaternary gravels whether in this or any other country.'[1] Earliest man, in fact, used the Thames as his highway, even if he did not, as we have already seen, have a hand in the fashioning of London. His stone implements of the palaeolithic type have been found in the City (Monkwell Street, Coleman Street, and Bishopsgate), in Gray's Inn Lane, accompanied by the remains of the elephant, in the Clerkenwell Road, Drury Lane, Jermyn Street,

[1] Evans *Stone Implements* 581

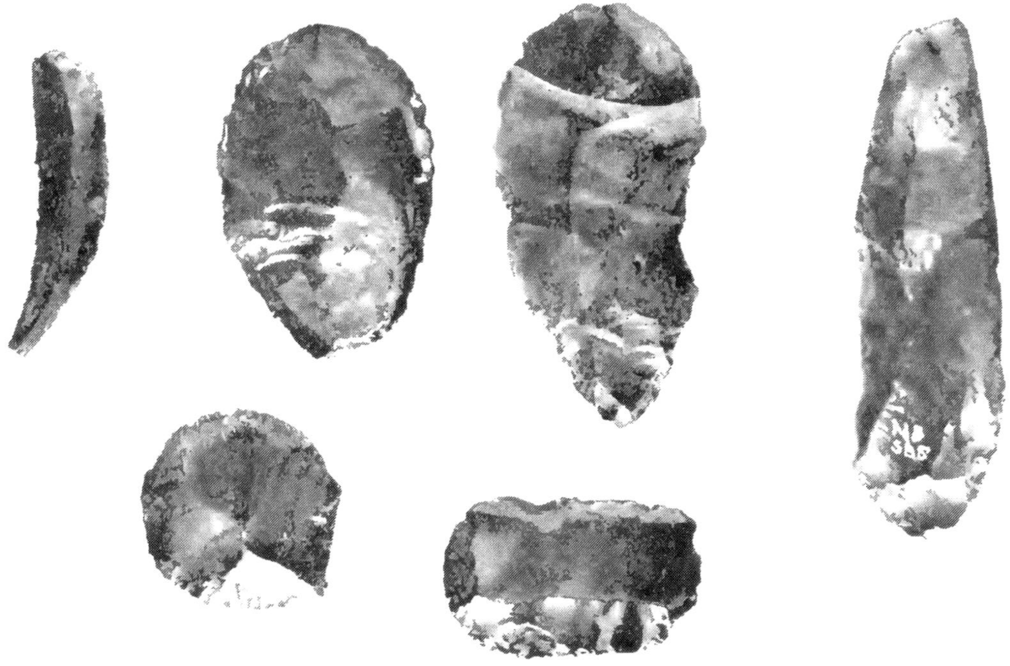

Flint Implements in the Guildhall Museum.

and Princes Street (Oxford Street).[1] Penetrating further
from the waters of the Thames, there have been found,
twenty-two feet below the surface in the gravel, implements of the oval type at Hackney Downs, a remarkably
well-formed implement at Highbury New Park, well
adapted for being held in the hand as a sort of knife
or chopper, and other remarkably fine implements in
London Fields, Dalston, Kingsland, Homerton, Lower
Clapton, Upper Clapton, Stamford Hill, Mildmay
Park, South Hornsey, Abney Park Cemetery, Stoke
Newington, and Shacklewell. This great area has
been called the palaeolithic floor by its discoverer,
Mr. Worthington Smith, and the implements have
been found side by side with the remains of wild
animals, such as the hyena, elephant, rhinoceros, and
others, whose broken bones, teeth, antlers, and tusks
abound.

At Stoke Newington the implements are as a rule
small. They consist of small and neat scrapers, knives
or chopping tools, knives made from flakes, flakes
unfashioned, but evidently used by man, and hammer
stones. Among special types, one implement of
quartzite was possibly made for ornament or amuse-
ment, or as a test of skill and dexterity, because its
manufacture was much more difficult than the ordinary tools of flint which were so abundantly made.[2]
A chopping tool, a good and massive example shows
by the straight part or back of the tool that it was
held in the hand for use while the semicircular edge
was used for chopping or hacking. Some specimens
of tools in an unfinished state are also among the

[1] Evans, *Stone Implements*, 582; *Catalogue of Guildhall Museum*, sect. 1.
[2] W. G. Smith, *Man the Primeval Savage*, 320–62.

Flint Implements in the Guildhall Museum.

Stoke Newington finds, speaking to us eloquently of the possible conditions of danger or despair which induced the workers to leave their task uncompleted, while an anvil stone, known by the distinct marks of hammering seen on some special parts of the stone, generally on a flat or flattish surface, and the small fabricator used for finishing off the larger implement, take us into the presence of the tool-worker.

This is the story from the palaeolithic floor at Stoke Newington. It is more or less repeated in those other parts of northern London which have been enumerated as containing the buried relics of earliest man on the site of London, and there is evidence of extensive workings of palaeolithic implements. At Acton, in the Criffield Road, Mr. J. Allen Brown discovered in an area not more than forty feet square more than 600 flakes and implements of the palaeolithic workers, showing emphatically the existence of a large settlement. In the bed of the river at Chelsea, Battersea, Wandsworth, Putney, and Hammersmith many specimens have from time to time been found, perhaps the relics of misfortune during the crossing of the river, when ill-equipped man had to meet not only human foes, with whom he was always at enmity, but animal foes who pressed upon him as their rightful prey. On the south side we get only sporadic finds, such as an implement and flake on Battersea Rise at the junction of the Grayshott Road and the Wandsworth Road, near Clapham Common; on East and West Hill, Wandsworth: at Lavender Hill, and at Lewisham.[1] These are the ovate palaeolithic implements.

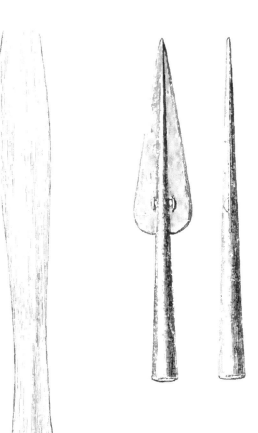

BRONZE AGE WEAPONS.
(By permission of Sir Arthur Ev

If all that these relics tell of the remotest past is
formulated into a story which the slight glimpses of
light permit us to make, it does not tell us of a future
London.   It is only the site of the future London that
yields the story.   The relics had been buried beneath
a geologic cataclysm which effectually blotted out the
human element when the arrival of new-comers from
the continent began a new and more continuous life.
The remains of these new folk are of stone, as of the old
folk, but they are fashioned differently.   Ages of workmanship had produced improvements.   Improvements
in culture mean improvements in social organization,
and improvements in social organization lead to closer
ties with different localities and the gradual adaptation
of local features to the needs and desires of man in his
stronger social conditions.   This new age of culture
and society was what is known as the neolithic.

The most striking thing about the neolithic finds is
that they occur nearer the surface, sometimes on the
surface, and in association with burials and other
indications of a settled life.   The principal finds in
London are from the Thames.   The most general of
the implements is a scraper, as it is called, which is
in some cases horseshoe-shaped or kite-shaped, in
others nearly circular.   They are only from $1\frac{1}{2}$ inches
to $2\frac{1}{2}$ inches in diameter and have a cutting edge on
one of the sides, the other side being for holding in
the hand, some being fashioned for the right hand and
others for the left hand   It is supposed that they
were principally used for scraping hides and preparing
leather, and they were probably also used for making
pins and other small articles of bone and perhaps for
fabricating arrow-heads   They have been found at

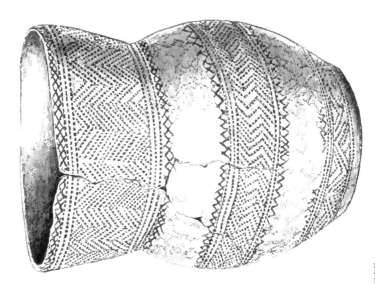

BRONZE AGE POTTERY.

From Greenwell's *British Barrows*.

Stoke Newington, but their discovery in London is naturally not extensive [1]

Their mere presence in small numbers, however, brings those who made them into touch with London. These people lived in communities having definite economic and social organization, and it is a question whether they witnessed the passing of the stone implement into the bronze or whether they had to meet a conquering people armed with bronze implements.

The possession of bronze implements implies a considerable advance in civilization. Bronze is an alloy, not a pure metal, and not only the instruments but the metal out of which they were formed had to be manufactured. The passing away of the stone-implement culture, and the formation of the bronze-implement culture, represent two distinct events with no connexion between the two. All the evidence seems to show that the earlier of the intruding Celtic peoples, who came to Britain in two great waves, were responsible for the introduction of the bronze implement. Finds of these implements are more difficult to classify than those of stone implements They perish more easily: they may be manufactured for ornamental or ceremonial use, after the age when they were universally used, and their presence in any excavated site does not necessarily determine the age of the site Still. there are some indications which cannot be mistaken. A helmet of hemispherical form tapering to a projection pierced above to receive a crest or ornament was found in Moorgate Street; and another found in the Thames near Waterloo Bridge had projecting horns and was ornamented with scroll work and red enamel. The latter, Sir John Evans pronounced to be of the late Celtic period.[1] These undoubtedly reveal to us the Celtic warrior. It is noticeable that the Thames has yielded several examples of bronze weapons of war. A portion of a sword blade with the scabbard end still in position, found in the river near Isleworth, a sheath end retaining a fragment of wood inside found near London, and another at Chelsea, are the most important. Daggers, weapons of a rapier shape, swords, sword hilts, spear heads, and ferrules for spear shafts have also come from the Thames. A class of implement known as palstaves, and designed to be fixed in some sort of haft, may have been used as a weapon of war, and these have been found in the Thames at London. Perhaps, however, the most interesting bronze war relic from the Thames at London is a fine shield 21 inches in diameter, with four rows of bosses about an inch in diameter and the same number of raised rings. There is at least one hole through the shield, which Sir John Evans thinks may have resulted from a spear thrust. Another shield $21\frac{1}{4}$ inches in diameter has a similar hole. Of objects which are not used for war we have only some brooches, socketed celts, chisels, sickles, and knives.

These finds are not enough to determine a definite place for London in the bronze age. But if Dr Montelius is correct in his classification of bronze age implements into chronological sequence, there is nearly certain evidence that the district of London has been occupied during the whole of that period, that is to say, from 2500 B.C. to 800 B.C. The barrow excavated at Teddington, showing traces of combustion extending

1 Anc. Bronze Implements, 350.

several feet round, with burnt sand and fragments of
charcoal. and in the centre a heap of calcined bones,
belongs to the earliest bronze age period,[1] and we are
justified in assuming that it was not the solitary instance of barrow interment in the London area, where,
as we have seen, examples of later bronze age objects
have been frequently discovered.

When we get beyond the bronze age we approach
the domain of history. The early iron age is represented by many objects discovered in London, most of
them weapons of war. swords, javelins, spear heads,
found near London Wall and in the Thames. Fibulae
and objects of bronze and bone are also found in
other parts of the city. Undoubtedly the great
dun, or stronghold, on the heights above the Fleet
river as tributary of the Thames. and partly surrounded by the lagoon waters of Finsbury, is the
significant feature of this period. Its remains bring
London into touch with similar remains which have
been found elsewhere in Britain, and on the Continent, and which help us therefore to estimate its
relationship to lake-dwelling culture. The details
conform to the general rule. It is unnecessary to
describe these details at great length. At the junction
of the Fleet river with the Thames. the first important
discovery was made by General Pitt-Rivers. He found
a number of piles, the decayed tops of which appeared
above the unexcavated portions of the peat, dotted
here and there over the whole of the cleared space.
Commencing on the south. a row of piles ran north and
south on the west side; to the right of these was
a curved row as if forming part of a ring: higher up

[1] Archaeologia, xxxvi 175; lxi 112.

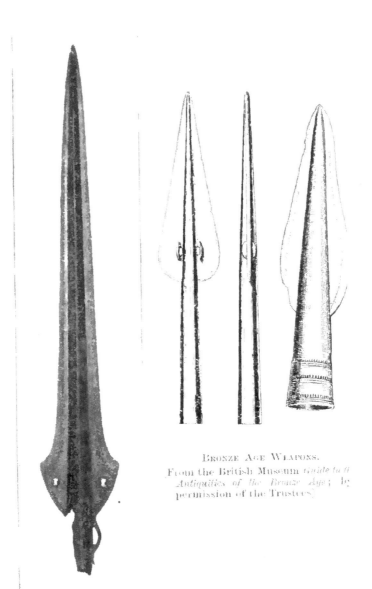

BRONZE AGE WEAPONS.
From the British Museum *Guide to the
Antiquities of the Bronze Age*; by
permission of the Trustees.

and running obliquely across the ground was a row of piles having a plank about an inch and half thick and a foot broad placed along the south face as if binding the piles together, to the left of these, another row of piles ran east and west; to the north-east again were several circular clusters of piles, not in rings but grouped in clusters. the piles being from eight to sixteen inches apart: to the left of this another row of piles and a plank two inches thick running north and south.[1]

Now the question is, what do these undoubtedly ancient pilings signify to the history of London? The piles were roughly cut as if with an axe and pointed square, and there was no trace of iron shoeing nor of metal fastenings on any of them. No remains of tiles or bricks were found associated with them, but two human skulls were found without any other remains of the skeletons.

The piles were evidently constructed for a super-structure, and this must have been made of wood. They are the foundations therefore of the river dwellings of the Celtic Britons, who built over the water as their brethren in Switzerland built, as other tribes in Britain and Ireland built, and this conclusion, arrived at by General Pitt-Rivers, has been confirmed by Mr. F. W. Reader in subsequent excavations in Finsbury, where the lagoon of waters to the north of the city was situated. Not only so, but the skulls also add their contribution to the story. The British tribesmen followed the practice of their age, and after a successful fight would ride home to their wives and children with the heads of their slain enemies at their saddle-bow, and which they placed as trophies in their houses.

---

[1] *Anthropological Review* v. p lxxi.

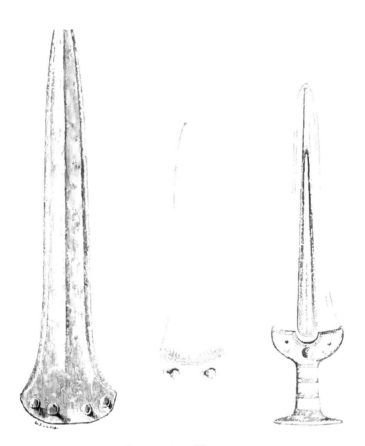

BRONZE AGE WEAPONS.

(From the British Museum *Guide to the Antiquities of the Bronze Age*; by
permission of the Trustees)

Nor is this all, if we may trust the observation of a well-known geologist of the middle of last century Mr. W. D Saull. Writing in 1845 a small pamphlet [1] devoted to the remains of the British aborigines, Mr. Saull declares that London was occupied by a people 'who raised and inhabited such rude dwellings as I have before described as extant in Yorkshire and several other places', and then goes on to state his observations 'made within the last few years'. Many deep cuttings were made for sewerage purposes in the principal streets of the city, and a subterranean passage was formed at the western end of Cheapside for that purpose. Whilst this was in progress, Mr. Saull 'constantly descended the shaft to examine the cuttings and the strata', and he discovered above the undisturbed gravel thin seams of ashes with small pieces of burnt wood lying in a concave form such as we might suppose occupied the lower part of the huts of the earliest inhabitants. These were from 18 to 22 feet below the present surface They were overlaid by the débris of the Roman period, consisting of the usual fragments of pottery, coins, and a quantity of concrete in variegated colours which had been used for the interior lining of their dwellings. This evidence seems well attested and very definite, pointing unquestionably to the hut-circle remains of the Celtic Londoners who occupied the high ground of their defensive stronghold. They tell us of the living Celtic tribesmen, and in the cinerary urns found in Lombard Street, Austin Friars, Cheapside London Wall, Minories.

---

[1] *Notitia Britanniae*, see pp 13-15. An illustration of the kind of dwelling here alluded to, from an example in the island of Lewis, may be seen in Mitchell's *Past in the Present*, p. 64.

A BRONZE BRITISH SHIELD FOUND IN THE TI
OF BATTLESEA

Fenchurch Street, Thames Street, Mark Lane, St. Martin's le Grand, Bishopsgate.[1] we have the concluding evidence of Celtic occupation.

Relics of this kind make us realize the two principal characteristics of Celtic London, and geologists have supplied its constructional features. Mr. Whitaker states that London is the first spot where vessels going up the river would find a narrow low-water channel close against ground of the most favourable kind for permanent occupation ground, indeed. yielding every advantage that could be wished for; and Mr. Reginald A. Smith has ably summarized these advantages. Above London there are only narrow strips of alluvium, the river flowing between gravel banks and necessarily keeping to a narrow channel Below London, however, the scene was far different from what we see to-day. The river flowed through mud plains covered with water at high tide only, and at low tide showing broad spreads of treacherous mud, as at Southend at the present day. Firm land was only touched at some of the bends in its course, as at Greenwich and Woolwich. The Lea valley may be taken as the limit of low ground on the north bank, and the river at the Custom House may well have been fordable at low tide, though dangerous to those not familiar with the crossing. Improbable as it may seem to any one standing on London Bridge, the shallow depth of the river is nevertheless supported by facts that came to light during the demolition of old London Bridge Sir G. B. Airy stated half a century ago that the depth of the foundations of the piers was good evidence of the depth of the river at old London Bridge. It appears from a published cross-

<hr>

[1] *Catalogue of Guildhall Museum*, 20-2.

section that the lowest part of the rubble, on which were laid the wooden sleepers supporting the masonry, was only from two to three feet below low water. It is certain he says, that this could not be higher than the general bed of the river, and it probably would be lower. Some channels naturally would be deeper than the general bed; and these, when the tide had risen a little, would make the operation of fording very dangerous.

The story is therefore fairly complete. At the foot of the steep rising represented by modern Ludgate Hill the homes of the Celtic Britons have been revealed to modern Londoners. At the summit of the rising, standing out of the surrounding waters, commanding the low lands around, was constructed the fortified stronghold to which the people and their cattle and belongings could retreat when necessity arose. Necessity often arose during the centuries of their occupation of the site which was first named London, Llyndun, the fort of the waters. But the greatest necessity of all came when the Roman soldiers, most probably the soldiers of Julius Caesar, the world-chieftain and leader, swarmed up the heights now represented by Ludgate Hill, to conquer the stronghold

CHAPTER III

OF THE PEOPLE WHO BEGAN THE MAKING OF LONDON

THERE was, then, no palaeolithic or neolithic London. The people who fashioned and used stone implements and weapons did not fashion a stronghold or a dwelling-place which was known to them as London. They roamed over its site, perhaps settled for a time on its heights perhaps defended themselves there or fled thither from elephant, rhinoceros, wolf, deer, and bear. But they did not settle there as a homeland They did not possess a homeland.

The incoming Celtic Britons were the first people who made a homeland of London. They were a virile race. Their round head, broadish face, full chin and rather heavy nose, their brown hair and hazel-grey eyes remain with us to this day. Their dash and bravery, their irresponsibility and generosity, their fierceness and friendliness made themselves known to Caesar and the later Roman generals who fought with them so often—so disastrously on a few great occasions and so successfully in the end.

They are still represented by the people in the neighbourhood of London, and, says Mr. Ripley, the explanation is simple. The Thames was closed to all later intrusions by the presence of London The fens on the north London on the south with dense forests in early times left the population of this district relatively at peace, and 'the marked island of brunetness just north of London', accompanied by a shorter stature, betoken a British lineage surviving to this day.[1]

Wonderful things have been said and surmised about these Celtic beginners of London. But the facts do not demand these wonders. Celtic Londoners were tribesmen with tribal civilization, tribal economy, and tribal methods of life. The tie was that of kinship not land or country, and kinship was largely the kinship by blood and more completely by religious rite and belief. There were no individuals in tribal society. What was affected by misfortune or by success was the kin. not the individual—a murdered kinsman had to be avenged by kinsmen, a successful undertaking was shared in by kinsmen. The tribal constitution allowed the tribal units to combine for a common purpose, to break up into its units again, to settle down upon a territory it had conquered, and to march out of a country of which it was no longer the master. It allowed of conquest and settlement, unsettlement and migration over and over again, and it always re-formed on the old lines with the old fact or theory of a blood kinship, and the old fact of a sacred tribal religion as the basis of its existence. If we would properly understand the tribalism which marked the occupation of Celtic London we should go to the tribalism of India, where the political civilization of modern England has been face to face with the tribal organization from which she herself had her beginning. These people had no cities or states, no life based absolutely upon a settled occupation of a definite country. They held the stronghold of London and were conquered there by the Romans and

¹ ...

those who escaped marched from London to Verulam or to some other stronghold and fought in their new home as strongly as they had done in their old one. It is somewhat doubtful which of the Celtic tribes held London. The Trinobantes held modern Essex, and Dr. Guest, a great authority, argues that the Lea was their western boundary, and Colchester the site of their stronghold. The Catuvellauni were west of them, and they extended up to the Colne valley, and there seems little doubt that it was these people who centred round London as their stronghold.[1]

Under the Celtic tribesmen were non-tribesmen, the conquered aborigines of the country, those neolithic folk who brought with them a knowledge of the cereals and of agriculture, who tilled the land, made the pottery and other objects of general use, and generally acted as the servants of the conquering tribesmen—servants with definite rules and rights within the tribal homestead but with no rights of marriage or of religion.

The influence of the tribal life of the Celts, whether in organization or in belief, could not have led to the foundations of a city. For that we must reckon with a wholly different influence by a different people and civilization The tribal stronghold of Celtic London was put on one side by the later influences, and Celtic London ceased to be.

It is particularly important to understand that the social organization of the Celts. both at the time when they met the Roman armies in Britain and after the Romans had left Britain, was tribal in form, not national It disposes of the various theories which

[1] Guest Origines Celticae ii 390 406

have been built up of there being a great London
city before the Romans came there, a city of palaces,
public buildings, residential magnificence, and organized governance, all of which is the creation of
twelfth-century chronicleis who translated Roman
remains into evidence of Celtic history.   The truth of
this condition of Celtic civilization is contained in the
evidence of Caesar and Tacitus for pre-Roman times
and in the remains of Celtic tribalism for post-Roman
times   The Welsh laws are the laws of tribesmen, not
of a nation, and they belong to post-Roman times.
They must have lived through Roman times, therefore, and been supported by a people whose social
organization was tribal.   It is not to the point to argue
that coming from Wales they come from an outskirt
and not from the centre of Roman Britain   Laws are
not applicable to special localities, but to special
peoples, and these laws of the Celtic Britons proclaim
in clear and definite fashion that the people who lived
under them were tribesmen, not citizens, held together
by ties of kinship and religion and not of territory
and state power.

The London that was made and the people who
made it in these earliest times were not, therefore, connected with those who were to come hereafter.   London
the Celtic stronghold is as completely separated from
London the city as any of the isolated Celtic strongholds in other parts of the country which stand out
as monuments of the past are separated from the
succeeding ages; and we must not, because of continuity
of occupation, think of continuity of history.   The
break-up of Celtic London did not arouse the attention
of history

CHAPTER IV

WHAT LONDON WAS TO CELTIC BRITONS

ALTHOUGH the evidence thus far shows London as a stronghold centre of the tribal life of the Celtic Britons. there is further evidence which brings it into a different relationship to the Celtic Britons.

In the first place we can gather up some facts connected with the religious cult of Celtic London which show it to have been sufficiently powerful to impress itself upon the Roman conquerors. The Romans were always ready to be impressed by the local divinities of their conquered territory, and there are many evidences of this, including some British examples [1] As Gibbon puts it, 'the various modes of worship which prevailed in the Roman world were all considered by the people as equally true, by the philosopher as equally false, and by the magistrate as equally useful' (cap. 11). It is owing to such doctrine as this that we can turn to the name of the Celtic god Lud, as well as to some strange rites which were incorporated in the ancient ritual of St. Paul's, and penetrate to the original Celtic worship.

Professor Rhys has investigated the worship of Lud, and concludes that it was a water worship [2] Lud as

[1] Mr. Warde Fowler has dealt with this subject in his *Religious Experience of the Roman People*; see particularly. Lecture X, what he says of the worship of Diana

[2] *Celtic Heathendom*. 125-33

god of the waters would exactly suit all we know about
the earliest site of London, and there is some indication of what this worship was from a parallel Celtic
worship on the Severn. That the name of Ludgate in
modern London contains the god-name Lud, is a fact,
therefore, which takes us back to the Celtic Britons in
London. Perhaps in the name of Mount Nod in
Wandsworth we may have another echo of the god
of the waters. Almost certainly the name of Belinus,
another Celtic god, is enshrined in Billingsgate.

There seems to be more than this The worship of
Lud, in whatever form it was accomplished, probably
took place on the site now occupied by St. Paul's
Cathedral. A temple of Diana stood there in Roman
times, and her worship included one feature which connected her with a water divinity. Animals, too, were
sacrificed to her, the principal one being the stag, and
many remains of stag horns and skulls have been found
on the site of St. Paul's. The church, moreover, had
a special stag ceremony A stag's head was fixed upon
a spear and conveyed about within the church with
great solemnity and sound of horns, and it was received
at the steps of the church by the priests in their
sacerdotal robes and with garlands of flowers upon
their heads. These facts are recorded by Camden, the
celebrated Tudor antiquary. They are not of Christian
origin, even though they may have been adopted into
the uses of the church, and they contain particulars
which without doubt take us back to Celtic worship in
London

We have next to proceed in another and very
significant direction. It has been noted that the ethnological evidence points to the persistence of a Celtic

population in the neighbourhood of London, and it is
not a little curious that in the place-name of Walworth
we have a definite record of the Wealas or British.
We may ask at this point whether the persistence of
a Celtic people near London has lent its aid to the
production of a Celtic view of London when London
itself had ceased to be Celtic.   The answer comes
from ancient traditions preserved in eleventh-century
chronicles, and from modern folklore preserved by
tradition, where there is a whole set of Welsh conceptions of London which, though not true to history, are
true as indications of the attitude of the Celtic Britons
towards London.   These conceptions proclaim that
London was a wonderland to the Celtic Britons, who
looked upon her buildings, her wealth, and her power
as the work of giant-men.

The group of legends found all over the country
relating to London Bridge and the treasure that
was to be found there, will help us to realize this.   An
examination and analysis of these legends make it
clear that we are in the presence of a remarkable
attitude, taken up by those who created the legends,
towards London Bridge.   It was a structure beyond
their ken.   It meant supernatural agency and perhaps
the sacrifice of a human being to the god of the Thames.
Clearly it could not have been the Roman builders,
designers, engineers, and masons who would have
believed such wonders   As clearly it must have been
the Britons who looked on and saw the structure taking
shape—trod its stone pathways after it had taken
shape.   It was a wonder to them, and we have in the
form in which that wonder was expressed and has
come down through the ages to modern times one of

the most fascinating glimpses at the work of the Romans in London. Indeed if Celtic myth is properly examined, there is much to show that it contains not the voice of the Celtic Britons concerning their own London, but of the greatness of London and its position in a civilization not theirs, and so much beyond theirs that it became a wonderland to them.

Slight though these remnants are, they serve a very important purpose therefore   They show not only the limitations of Celtic London but the reality of early Roman London. Celtic worship was incorporated in Roman worship, and had in this fashion received a new life Celtic tradition relates to an external Roman London, and proves that the Celts of London, like the Celts in the rest of Britain, were not citizens, not builders of a city, not founders of a state. They did not help in the making of London therefore. These Celtic remains are thus of supreme importance to the understanding of the beginnings of London, and not only the beginning, but also the essential feature of continuity. The material remains take us to the primitive tribal hut and the cinerary urn, buried beneath the Roman city. The worship and the tradition take us to the living Roman city The appeal in both cases therefore is entirely to Roman London.

It is obvious that we are entitled to draw two conclusions from this double set of facts   The first is that London was not only a defensive stronghold of the Celts, but, as the centre of a religious cult, possessed the full life of the Celtic tribesmen. The second conclusion is that the new London of the Romans entirely replaced Celtic London for the Celtic tradition

J86 16

expresses the operation of the changed conditions in terms which belong to the period during which the changes were being effected. This makes it abundantly clear that Roman London with its continuous tradition must have had a continuous life, threading out no doubt at certain times into a narrow compass, but never entirely broken. It is to this significant fact of continuity that I shall appeal throughout the succeeding pages of our study. I shall urge that if we never lose sight of Celtic worship and tradition preserved from Roman London, we cannot safely include in the mere silence of Anglo-Saxon history a decayed and desolate city and I shall ask that the undoubted inheritance by modern London from Roman London which we now proceed to examine may be tested by this underlying stratum of continuity.

CHAPTER V

THE ROMANS IN LONDON

IF it is correct to conclude, from the scanty evidence
at command, that London was the stronghold of the
Celtic Britons which Julius Caesar attacked and
captured in his second invasion of Britain, it marks
the beginning of the real history of London It is
true this episode did not lead directly to occupation,
but it began the Roman policy of adding Britain to
the empire. Julius Caesar began his conquest, such as
it was, in the year 55 B.C, and ninety-eight years
later, in A.D. 43. the Roman general, Aulus Plautius,
landed in Britain. He also made his way first of all to
the stronghold on the Thames. and this fact seems con-
firmatory of the direction of the earlier expedition.
It was a strategic point. Dr. Guest has described the
scene that met the Romans. 'When the Romans
came down the Watling Street to the neighbourhood
of London they saw before them a wide expanse of
marsh and mudbank which twice every day assumed
the character of an estuary sufficiently large to excuse
if not to justify the statement in Dio Cassius that the
river there emptied itself into the ocean. No dykes
then retained the water within certain limits. One
arm of the great wash stretched northwards up
the valley of the Lea, and the other westwards
down the valley of the Thames The individual
character of the rivers was lost; the Romans saw only

one sheet of water before them and they gave it the
name of the river which mainly contributed to form
it.' Aulus Plautius vainly endeavoured to cross these
marshes, and, withdrawing his troops, encamped them
somewhere in the neighbourhood. Dr. Guest believes
this somewhere to have been London. 'At London,'
he says, ' the Roman general was able both to watch his
enemy and to secure the conquests he had made, while
his ships could supply him with all the necessaries he
required. When in the autumn of the year 43 he
drew the lines of communication round his camp,
I believe he founded the present metropolis of Britain.'[1]

In the main this seems to be the correct interpretation of the scanty notices of these great events, though
Dr Guest evidently infers, and in another place argues,
that a Celtic *oppidum*, named London, did not exist,
and that therefore Plautius was in reality the founder
of the site as an occupation place. Except for this,
Dr. Guest's account meets the case. It takes us as far
as A D. 61, when London is first mentioned in history,
namely. by Tacitus, in describing the events of that
year. It was a memorable year. Rome was busy in
taking her first steps towards making Britain a province
of the Empire. London was busy with the first results
of this, and was becoming a centre of commerce. It
has been questioned whether this great uprise of
London could have been accomplished in the short
period of the Roman occupation. But there can be
no doubt it was the Roman occupation which produced
such a result. More than this, it was only the Roman
occupation which at that period could have produced
it London was used as a Roman camp. and had

[1] *Origines Celticae* ii 405

grown from a camp to a commercial centre   It was on
the Roman highway and was thus connected with the
Roman world   Commerce would originate with the
military occupation, and would extend in consequence
of it.   There is no question about the fact   There can
be no question about the cause.

It is clear that the Romans had not fortified it as
a town, only as a camp.   The commercial parts had
spread outside the camp, and these parts were open to
the country.   Now it happens that we can begin our
knowledge of Roman London by a gleam of light
coming to us from the story of Boudicca's revolt.
The abandonment of London by the Roman general
Suetonius was a necessity of the military situation,
and, says Tacitus, 'he resolved to save the province
as a whole by the sacrifice of that one city.   Unmoved
by the tears and entreaties of the inhabitants, he gave
the signal to march, receiving within his lines all that
could come with him ; those who remained behind,
whether through weakness of sex or age or from
attachment to the place, were massacred by the enemy. [1]

We need not linger over the massacre, for it was
much the same as such events have always been   But
I want to call attention to the fact that black as are the
events which enclose the first mention of London in
history, there is also the brightest gleam of sunshine.
There were Londoners even in A D. 61 who were
attached to the place—an attachment which is also
recorded in the Welsh legend of King Lludd.   And
these Londoners were Roman Londoners.   It is a great
historic scene, pregnant with events, and Roman Lundinium was gutted with the blood of proud Londoners

1 Tacitus Annals xiv cap 33

London was recovered from this disaster, and her Roman masters rebuilt her with a wall to take in the larger area necessary for her commerce, and endowed her with a new name, Augusta. The significance of these facts is very great. It is difficult to give a date to the walls which enclosed the larger London, but everything points to an early date. They made London the largest Roman city in the British province of the Roman empire, and that it was given a special Roman name is enough to signify its importance in the Roman system of government.

The Roman name did not last, and I think the replacing of the name, Augusta, by the former name, London, introduces us to an interesting bit of history. Tacitus is not the kind of writer to state anything for mere rhetorical purposes, and his sentence implying what the Londoners of the first century thought of their defended camp and its undefended externals, coupled with its new name of Augusta, leads one to believe that the newly extended Augusta might have preserved the older London in some sort of traditional reverence, just as Romans retained a religious reverence for the original Rome.

There are indications of this. The older Roman London may be traced from the boundaries of the wards and parishes, which reveal a rough parallelogram, one of whose sides would be by the river between Billingsgate and Dowgate Hill, the other being represented practically by Cheapside. This parallelogram is the exact site which would fit in with the known facts of the Roman camp before the rebuilding of the city.

There is next to note the interesting fact, recently pointed out by Mr Reginald A. Smith, that remains

exist of an ancient road running east and west on the
brow of the hill just above what is now London Bridge
When that road was first engineered we can only surmise, but it was certainly built or rebuilt by the Romans.
An entire section of it was made and published in
1833 during alterations for the bridge-approach in
what is now Cannon Street. A gravel road 16 feet
wide, supported by two walls $7\frac{1}{2}$ feet high, was found
about 3 feet below the modern roadway, pointing to
London Stone on the west and apparently to Aldgate
on the east, but it has not been traced east of Gracechurch Street. Narrower by 8 feet than Watling Street,
as discovered in Edgware Road, it lacked the layer of
flints that distinguished the Roman military roads;
but there is no doubt of its Roman construction. as
the containing walls have bands of the familiar tiles
between stages of Kentish ragstone.[1]

If we fix the western boundary of this area as con-
terminous with that of the parish of St. Swithin, we
find that on this boundary originally stood London
Stone, and immediately adjoining it is the parish of
St. Martin Pomroy. Now London Stone has always
been a remarkable centre of rites, ceremonies, and
traditions, which show it to have been held in reverence through the centuries. It stood on the western
extremity of the first Roman London, which may
perhaps point to it as one of the stone sides of the
gateway which led to the pomerium ; and if the Roman
word for this sacred institution is still preserved in the
second name of the City parish, Pomroy, we may allow
the suggestion that in these two facts, so remarkable
in combination, is contained evidence of the reverence

1 See Lethaby : &c. 108 to 602

for the oldest London having been preserved by the Romans of Augusta. This point is greatly helped by the persistence of the name of London and its final conquest over that of Augusta Ammianus Marcellinus, who wrote about A. D. 380, calls London simply Augusta. The Ravenna geographer of the seventh century calls it Lundinium Augusta If this indicates the growing restoration of the original name it is possible to suggest that it was preserved by the oldest part of the city, that part to which Tacitus refers as receiving the attachment of its inhabitants. It would revive still more strongly after the departure of the Romans and during the independence of the city in the period when the Celts were withstanding the incoming Saxons. In a word, I think the preservation of the name of London is part of the evidence for the preservation of the Roman London of earliest times as an institutional part of the greater Roman London.

I will now turn to the later and larger Roman city, and I note the significance of the tradition which has just been recorded as evidence of the fact that the Romans of London behaved as they behaved in any of the daughter cities in Gaul, Spain, or Italy, and even Rome herself. Indeed, it is important to bear in mind that Roman London must always be considered from the point of view of its position as a city of the Roman empire, not as a city of Britain. It was dependent upon Rome for its military position, its institutions, and its commercial greatness. Its position has to be measured by these facts, and not by its geographical position in Britain. The principal Roman roadways converged to it. Of the fifteen great road routes mentioned in the Antonine itinerary no less than

LONDON STONE, CANNON STREET.

eight converge upon London, and it is important to note that the *iter Britanniarum* is prefaced by a statement of the distance from Gessoricum (Boulogne) to Portus Ritupis (Richborough), thus showing that the road system of Britain was part of the road system of the empire.[1]

Travellers from London who want to proceed along the best and most direct roads must to this day take one of the Roman roads which connected London with the rest of Roman Britain and with the continental empire of Rome. The roads from London to the south lead to Richborough, the Roman Ritupis, Dover (Dubris), and Lymne (Lemanis). We have in modern days to make our way to Blackheath to save being lost in the maze of streets which cover the area from the Thames far into South London. Yet in this maze there are streets which are fragments of the ancient Roman *iter*. Near London Bridge, on the south side, is a street called Stony Street, a sure indication of an ancient Roman road, and Mr. Loftie has acutely pointed out that the Watling Street of London would, if continued in its original direction, have ended at the Thames just opposite where Stony Street on the south begins (*Hist. London*, i. 28). Stony Street would have joined the main Roman road where the present Old Kent Road begins its course. This road is the Roman road and proceeds straight to New Cross, where it is lost amidst a maze of streets. The ancient road reappears, however, when Blackheath is gained. From Shooter's Hill to Swanscombe there is a straight road for 10½ miles through Crayford (the

<hr />

[1] Gibbon, *Decline and Fall*, edit Bury, i 50, states the general position with his usual brilliancy

important Roman site which, as we shall see, marked the southern limits of the territorium of Roman London), to Dartford, Northfleet, and Rochester. Before reaching Northfleet there is a bend in the road, and here considerable remains of a Roman town have been discovered. On the Strood side of the river Mr. George Payne has found remains of the actual Roman road, paved and showing the ruts on the paving (*Arch. Cantiana*, xxiii). From Rochester the road proceeds to Canterbury through Sittingbourne, and from thence to Dover in almost one continued straight line The western road from London takes us through a most interesting part of Roman Britain, with one town, Silchester, left among the green fields undestroyed in its foundations, and now patiently excavated plot by plot throughout the entire area within the still extant walls. The route is fixed by the great western road leading direct to Staines, the Pontes of the Romans, thence to Silchester (Calleva Attrebatum). The road from Calleva branches into three one of them proceeding to Exeter, a second to Bath, and a third to Gloucester and Monmouth. The north-western route goes down the Edgware Road—the high sides on the north of Maida Vale have been said to be the remains of the Roman protective banks—to Elstree, which is perhaps the Sulloniacae of the Romans, thence to Verulamium (near St. Albans), still with its walls nearly extant enclosing the city remains beneath green fields, thence to Wroxeter and branching to Lincoln. The great road to the north goes to York and Carlisle. It first turned eastwards to Caesaromagum (Chelmsford), passing from London at Old Ford, then to Camulodunum (Colchester) whose Roman walls are still partly extant, and whose castle is built of Roman materials, thence northwards. These roadways show that the Romans of London lived their life as Romans everywhere did, ever looking to their mother city on the Tiber as the source of all their prosperity and hope.

To understand the work of the Romans of London, then, apart from its constructive results, we must go to Roman sources, and no doubt all that is to be gathered about the daily life and habits of the Romans from the histories, inscriptions, and poems would apply with but slight variation in matters of detail to those of them who lived either permanently or for a time in London. Only very occasionally is the curtain drawn aside for us to be able to catch an actual glimpse. At the time when military usurpation of the title and position of the Emperor had occurred, two of our own chroniclers, Geoffrey of Monmouth and Matthew of Westminster, write as if they were at least preserving an accepted tradition that the Britons attacked the city and were met by Levius Gallus, 'who had collected the rest of the Romans in the city,' on which occasion the Britons were victorious. This event, however, refers to the reign of Allectus, the murderer of Carausius, in A.D 293. He was defeated and slain by Constantius, who followed up his victory by marching to London, whither the soldiers of Allectus had fled. They were engaged in sacking the city and were slaughtered in the streets. One other event is depicted by Ammianus Marcellinus in describing the successes of Theodosius in A.D. 368. He marched from Richborough to London, 'an ancient town called of late years Augusta . . . . . . He entered with triumph into the city, which a short time before had been plunged in the greatest distress, and was

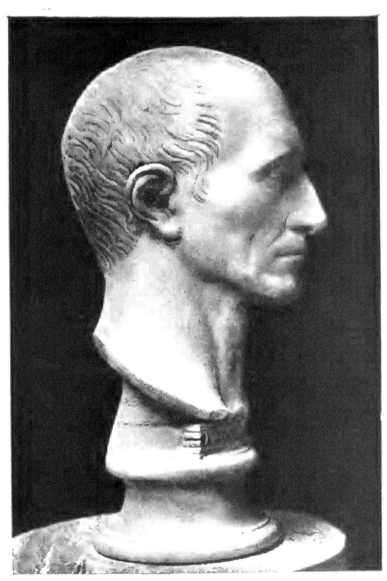

now suddenly called to life by the salvation which had so unexpectedly appeared '

We may picture if we will these rough doings in the most remote part of the Roman empire much in the same way as they occur in our own empire of to-day. They are particularly interesting to us because of one very important relic of this part of London history which has only recently been discovered. It is a Roman boat, the only one ever discovered in Britain, found under 14 feet of silted Thames mud and débris, on the site of the new County Hall at the foot of Westminster Bridge. The vessel was about 60 feet long and was built for sailing. Without attempting to describe it in detail, one or two facts are of great interest. A large hole occurs near the bows, and below the vessel and 2 feet away from the hole a portion of the mast was found, measuring 2 ft 5 in. long and 10 in in diameter, from which it may be fairly concluded that the breaking of the mast was due to some violent cause   In this connexion another find is of considerable importance. It consists of several large rounded stones, about 3 lb. in weight, each one of which was partially embedded in a strake. indicating that it must have been thrown from a considerable height.   Such stones as these were used in Roman warfare, and we have therefore a series of connected facts which indicate that the boat was destroyed by a definite attack which must have included the correlative of a definite defence.   But attack and defence mean battle   What struggle this vessel comes from, and what part it took, it is impossible to say. but turning to the objects found in the vessel we have a very important indication of

BRITANNIA (BOADICEA).

From the Statue at Westminster Bridge

date. These are the coins, of which there were three, one of Tetricus the Elder, A.D. 268–73, found beneath the rib nearest the bows, one of Carausius, A.D. 286–93, and one of Allectus, A.D. 293–6. The first is a Gaulish coin, the two latter are British, and they extend our view of the historical setting of this find by the suggestion that the vessel came over from Gaul, and that it ceased to be used after the reign of Allectus. This brings us back again to the campaign of Constantius against Allectus, which ended at London, and the conclusion seems irresistible that this boat was used in the defence of the city by the soldiers of Allectus It was used unsuccessfully, as the evidence produced from it clearly shows. That it was in actual use at the time of its destruction may be gathered from the fact that portions of leather footwear were found in the boat, together with various pieces of pottery. The stage from occupation to destruction therefore must have been a short one. It probably means that this was one of Allectus's vessels that endeavoured to escape from the fight at London but was overtaken and destroyed

These things tell us of the stress. Other things tell us of the peace. The coins of the Constantine family bear the inscription P. LON. or M. LON., an indication certainly of the presence of a mint in London ; and despite the fact that Roman London can only be dug into whenever the events of modern London have allowed or necessitated that course, we may pick our way amidst the tesselated pavements, the pottery, the inscribed stones, the sculptures, the weapons, implements and coins, and other objects which have from time to time been discovered, for the rebuilding of the evidence of the life that went on there. The list of smaller objects is remarkable   Brooches, hairpins, combs, ear-picks, tweezers, mirrors, pendants and ear-rings, armlets, finger rings, gems, dress fasteners bodkins and needles, shoes and sandals, balances scales, bowls, fish-hooks, forks, knives, spoons, ladles, strainers. spinning and weaving implements surgical instruments, musical instruments, writing implements, lamps, tools, mechanical requisites, bolts, cramps, nails, bells. chains, locks and keys. bowls, cups and dishes, horse furniture.   All this would take us to Roman ideals and habits, to Roman commerce, Roman government and law.

It seems clear, then, that scattered though the evidence is, and difficult as it is to gather together and estimate the value of its various parts, it will repay examination if considered on broad lines and taken as a whole.   As a starting-point it enables us to come into definite touch with the Romans of London, those far-off people who began the making of our city for us, for we can think of the Roman Londoner as proud of his city, proud of its inner area, the seat of a religious cult adopted from the conquered Celts, sacred perhaps to those who were slaughtered there by Boudicca; proud of its larger area, its life, its commerce, and its power

\

CHAPTER VI

ROMAN LONDON

THE Roman Londoner has left conciete relics of his life in Roman London. They are now principally contained in our museums—the British Museum and the Guildhall Museum. But portions of its Great Wall remain *in situ*. The mediaeval wall of London was built on the Roman foundations and sometimes incorporated portions of the Roman Wall itself, and the modern Londoner may still walk along streets which correctly define the limits of Roman London within the walls. Opposite Finsbury Circus, in obscure courts and cellars from the Tower to Cripplegate, at Houndsditch, at Old Bailey, in Warwick Lane, Friday Street, Knightrider Street, Newgate Street, Christ's Hospital, important fragments have been found, and only in August, 1908 a large portion was discovered in America Square during excavations there. The bastion in Cripplegate churchyard and the section in London Wall are the only portions now remaining above ground, except fragments here and there built into modern structures

If all the constructional remains of Roman London which have been discovered during the period when professional or antiquarian interest has existed had been properly preserved and exhibited there would be enough to demonstrate the ordered life of the Roman city Scattered as they are, they tell us this much, and it is

not necessary to describe them in detail here. It
is enough to know that they rival in comparison the
remains found in Britain on other Roman sites. London
is the one place in our island, says Mr. Haverfield,
which has yielded Roman objects of artistic merit in
real abundance [1]

It is far more necessary to understand the extra-
mural position of Roman London. Roman cities were
never bounded by their walls. There was first the
pomerium, a sacred belt of land extending right round
the walls, upon which no buildings could be erected.
Secondly, there was the territorium, the vast expanse
of lands upon which the city depended for its agri-
cultural produce, and in which the richer citizens
built their villas and their rural homes. These important adjuncts to a Roman city must not be ignored.
The city dominated the entire area, was lord over the
entire area, and the limit of its jurisdiction was therefore far beyond the walls of the city proper. That
London possessed both these adjuncts is proved by the
remains of them which have survived in later ages, and
the map of Roman London is never correct unless it
shows the city in the midst of its territorium.

The pomerium of London Augusta is probably represented by the ring of wards without the walls which
are to this day included in the area of the city and
extend without a break round the entire wall. This
extension beyond the walls has no known historical
origin, except so far as it is represented by the
covering in of the ditch outside the wall. This is
only a small portion of the outside ring, and it is

[1] *Archaeologia*, lx 43.   See the *Catalogue of the Guildhall Museum*,
25-119

therefore allowable to conclude that the main portion of it comes with the walls from Roman times and represents the pomerium of the city.

It is not possible to show the exact extent of the territorium of London, but it must be remembered that Silchester on the west, Verulam on the north, Colchester on the east, and Rochester on the south are the sites of important Roman cities, each of which no doubt had its territorium. And when we add to this the stretches of undeveloped forest or marshland, there seems warrant for saying that the territorium of London practically met the territoria of these other Roman cities. This alone would take us far towards the probable limits of the London territorium. These limits are, however, more precisely indicated by archaeological and historical evidence. At Crayford on the south, Wimbledon on the south-west, Staines on the west, Hampstead on the north, and Old Ford on the east, there are remains of singular importance in this connexion, and the conclusion is irresistible that they indicate the official boundaries of Roman London.

In point of fact London citizenship has always possessed special rights within the area which must have been the territorium of the Roman city. The sheriff of the city exercised his powers over the whole of Middlesex; the right of hunting by the citizens extended as far as the Chilterns and into Middlesex, Surrey and Kent; the jurisdiction over the Thames extended up to Staines; the Mile End from the eastern gate of the city, preserved to this day in the parish name, was not only the place of execution of city criminals, but the gathering ground of the city's army. Facts such as these can only be adequately accounted

for if we reckon them as relics of ancient rights in the territorium

The territorium contained the amphitheatre of London, a well-recognized feature of Roman city life. Some speculation has occurred as to the site of the London amphitheatre, and it has generally been looked for on the north of the Thames. But there is evidence that it was situated on the south. The Roman amphitheatres of some towns were continued in use. as at Cirencester, for English and mediaeval sport , and there is a famous site on the Southwark side of London known as the Bear Garden, used in its last stage as a theatre, but formerly, as its name implies, as a place for the sport of baiting bears. Up to this point. by comparison only with other places. we might surmise that this was a possible site of the London amphitheatre. at all events in the latest Roman period, when Southwark was undoubtedly an occupied suburb But we can go beyond the evidence from comparison to evidence from the site itself, for there have been found there the gladiators' trident, a sort of three-pointed lance which was used in the amphitheatre.

The territorium contained, too, country residences of the London magnates. The bath still *in situ* in the Strand belonged originally to a Roman villa or house. Pavements have been found at Westminster, and somewhat more extensive remains at Greenwich. The Greenwich remains are very interesting. Though there can be little doubt that there has been a building on the site, hardly any parts of it, beyond the small piece of coarse pavement, were discovered when they were excavated in 1902. The indication of walls or foundations are of the slightest ; but the quantities of

roofing tiles and rough building stones in a confused
mass over the ground probably indicate that the
walls were levelled. So far as the coins already
found give a date, it would be in the fourth century.
The objects of interest discovered may be enumerated
Floor of room, tessera partially intact, and remains
of hypocaust; twenty-three coins dating A.D. 79 to
A.D 403, two pieces of marble with partial inscription,
two pieces of bone beautifully carved; a large quantity
of broken pottery, including Samian, Upchurch, black
New Forest, and red; whetstone and pestle; part of
mortuary; various specimens of glass; bronze hinges,
safety pin, and ornaments; iron key, hair-pin (supposed), number of nails, staples, &c., bones not yet
recognized; antlers of red deer showing marks of
sawing, wall stucco in abundance; charcoal and
ballast; tiles (roofing and others); oolite slabs. Kings-
bury, just beyond Willesden, has considerable Roman
remains, and the walls of the church there are probably
of Roman workmanship. All this indicates not only
prosperity but peace, and peace was obtained from the
power possessed and wielded by the city.

Within this large stretch of territory attached to the
city there were no settlements—no towns or villages or
local communities, and it is this fact which empha-
sizes its character as the territorium of a great city. It
consisted of the cultivated lands of the conquered
country, and was worked by the enslaved conquered
people for the benefit of the city to which it
belonged. The Romans dealt with it in an ordered
and scientific way. Their surveyors divided it into
square plots of 120 perches each way, intersected it by
a system of roads all communicating with the city the

whole area being thus devoted to the purposes of
the city. Mr. Montagu Sharpe has studied the lands
of Middlesex and has discovered, even in modern
boundaries, clear traces of the centuriation of the
Romans, while Mr. Reginald A. Smith has turned to
the road system all round London and, with a daring
which is unusual in archaeological research, has pronounced the existence of Roman roads which exactly
fit in with the requirements of the Roman surveyors.

The time came when Roman London had to stand
without the support of Imperial Rome. In A. D. 410
the Roman empire was sore pressed by the tribes who
closed in upon her on all sides, and the Emperor
Honorius wrote letters to the cities of Britain, urging
them to provide for their own safety The importance
of this event is that it shows the centre of Roman
government to have been the cities. There was then
no British state, not even the beginnings of a British
state. The tribal Celtic Britons could not, and the
Romans did not. form Britain into a self-governed
state, and when London received the imperial script
she looked after her own interests independently of
all other parts of the country, whether cities or tribal
lands.

I think she assumed the position of city-state for
which her Roman organization and experience so
pre-eminently fitted her. The external sovereignty
of the empire having been thrown off, she would stand
revealed as the city-state, ready with all the forms and
traditions to take a place of independence in any new
form of state-government which might be developed.
How independently she behaved is indicated in one
or two ways. When the Roman general Artonius

allied himself to the Celtic Britons to fight against
the incoming Saxons, and began that brilliant series
of victories which was to make of him a British king,
the great hero of Celtic tradition and the King Arthur
of romance, he was crowned king at Caerleon and again
at Silchester. But London accepted no king from these
sister cities, and so we find that Arthur was crowned
also at London. This is significant of the independence
of Roman London during the period of the severe
struggle against the Anglo-Saxons ; and it is followed
by a correspondingly significant fact when Anglo-
Saxon kings had assumed the position of Bretwalda, that
is, sovereign of both the Anglo-Saxon and the British
people, namely, that there was a sub-king, sub-regulo,
of London This title had a long range It is referred
to in Welsh tradition when Bran, son of Llyr, · was
crowned king of this island and he was exalted from
the crown of London.' That this is not unreal tradition is shown by the parallel reference by the great
Welsh lawgiver, Howel Dha, in the early tenth
century, and again in the Scandinavian saga, the
Heimskringla of the twelfth century. We cannot
miss all that this means in the story of London's
independence or semi-independence after the Roman
imperial sovereignty had left her to fight her own
way. It is indicative of two things, the recognition of
London independence and a British appeal to a powerful city organized both for civil and military purposes.
London, therefore, naturally assumed the position of
city-state Her organization from Rome would qualify
her for that position if occasion arose. It arose, I think,
when Rome left the cities of Britain to fight against
the northern foe London was, however a city-state

with a difference. In course of time different stages of an outside sovereignty to which London had to bow were created. The struggle from this state of things will be outlined in the following pages. but the point we have reached now is important, for it brings us to the city-state of London as an institution of the land, and it is only from this standpoint that we can understand her later history.

CHAPTER VII

WHAT ROMAN LONDON LEFT TO LATER LONDON

LONDON was not the capital city of a state after it had ceased to be a city of the Roman empire If it was anything it was a petty state itself. A British state was not formed out of the relics of the Roman provincial government of Britain. It was not formed out of the tribal government of the British Celts or the tribal government of the Anglo-Saxons in Britain. And when out of the silence of both Celtic and Anglo-Saxon history London once more emerges, we find it still an organized city community, still powerful and strong, still able to defend itself and to give help towards the defence of the growing, but unformed English nation. It could not have derived its organization, its power, and its strength either from British or from English sources. for neither British nor English polity lent itself to the foundation of cities. There is therefore only one source from which it could have secured its position as a city in an unformed state, and this source was its heritage as a Roman institution. And if it kept this intact or practically intact during the troublous times of Anglo-Saxon conquest, it must have used it during the times of Anglo-Saxon settlement, and must have handed much of it on to later times when it took its place as the capital city of England.

There is a whole group of facts, archaeological, historical. legal, and constitutional, which go to prove this position. They must be taken together, and not singly. Their cumulative value, not their separate significance, must be considered. It is not an accident, but a point of scientific importance, that we can call upon a series of correlated facts for evidence, a series the elements of which are not only related to each other and consistent with each other, but which could have come from no other source than the Roman organization of London.

We have already dealt to some extent with the archaeological evidence, and we have suggested that the evidence of Celtic tradition assists this by its evident traces of mythic wonder which were laid open to the Celtic Britons when London, detached from the Roman empire, was attached as ally to the Celtic chieftains who were defending their country from the Anglo-Saxon conquerors.

If early London was not a capital city, it has always been an empire city- a city of two empires, two of the greatest empires the world has ever seen. She first of all grew to greatness as a city of that terrible but magnificent empire—Rome. She has grown to a more magnificent greatness as the capital city of the British empire If I attempt to sketch out the connecting links between Roman Lundinium and English London, and then attempt to sketch the contrast between the two Londons, 1 shall, of course, give an incomplete picture, but 1 think I shall give an instructive one. I think I shall give what has not hitherto been understood of London history, and the mere statement of a misunderstood phase of historical evolution is a step towards the complete story which some day will assuredly be written.

I cannot do better than begin with a contrast. Roman London appears so quickly among the first results of the Roman conquest of Britain that historians have been induced to turn to other sources than Rome to account for her position. English London appears to emerge so slowly from the conflicts and settlement of Anglo-Saxon times that historians are wont to assume an entire break with her earlier existence. And yet this contrast is in absolute keeping with the events which belong to both periods. The rapid growth of Roman London is the growth of a city naturally endowed when the fullest opportunity is afforded for growth. She was the Chicago or the Winnipeg of ancient days. The slow development of English London is the development of an institution not in keeping with the institutions with which it was surrounded. The rapid growth of Roman London was due to London herself—to her place on the Thames, to her connexion by roads with the continental cities and with Rome, to the commerce which made her the emporium of Western Europe. The uprising of English London was due to the genius of that greatest of English monarchs—Ælfred the Great—who, recognizing her strategical importance in the great contest that was before him, recognizing too the nationality awaiting the touch of genius to make it burst forth put on one side the tribal polity of his people and stood out for an English military power and an English state government. This contrast between Roman Lundinium and English London ends with a parallel, and a parallel of some importance. Boudicca had sacked the first

Roman London and had massacred its inhabitants.
The Romans answered by building the defending walls
of the second Roman London so as to include the
whole area which her commerce demanded. The
English king came to the London of his age, recognized in the half-destroyed walls the means of a great
defence against Danes and Norsemen, and once more
surrounded the city with its wall, built of the old
Roman material, and on exactly the Roman site.
Ælfred only restored what some great Roman had
constructed. Both depended upon the Roman defences
of London for a defence of the country.

I think these contrasts and this parallel are all-
important. They supply the key-note of history—the
key-note of London as an imperial city. Let us take
our stand by King Ælfred when in the year 886 he
surveyed the city and decided to use it for defence—
let us, if we can, try to see what he saw and as he saw
it. The Anglo-Saxon Chronicle records the facts—
'King Ælfred occupied London, and all the English
race submitted to him which was free from the thral-
dom of the Danish men, and then he entrusted the
town to the keeping of Æthelred aldorman.' Twelve
years later, that is in 898, there was a formal conference
at Chelsea between Ælfred, Æthered, Æthelflaed, and
Archbishop Plegmund on the fortifications of London
(Plummer's *Alfred*, 111, quoting Birch, No 577), and
Asser's *Life of Alfred* expands the record of his doings
in London by stating that 'he honourably rebuilt
(*restauravit*) the city of London and made it again
habitable (*et habitabilem fecit*). He gave it into the
custody of his son-in-law Æthered, earl of Mercia,
to which king all the Angles and Saxons who before

had been dispersed everywhere or were in captivity
with the pagans voluntarily turned and submitted
themselves to his dominion'.

These and a few other meagre references are all that
remains to us of the historical record of this event
As Mr. Stevenson points out, Asser was probably
describing what he actually saw, and it comes to this.
that the city was in such a condition that its restoration as a strategic defence of southern Britain was
quickly accomplished. But we may picture, if we
will, much more than this by understanding what
remained of a citizen-life of London after Ælfred's
time. That which remained in after years for us
to discover must have existed for Ælfred to see,
that which Ælfred saw must have been more extensive. more perfect, than the fragments which have
survived not only the necessary wear and tear of
succeeding centuries, but also the senseless destruction
by ignorant or indifferent Londoners I think, therefore, that if we take our stand by the great king, and
endeavour to see in imagination what he must have
seen in fact, we shall touch a momentous period in
London history—a period when the coming Anglo-
Saxon made his appeal to the departing Roman, when
the London of the Roman empire yielded up her best
to the London of the English. It is the period when
London, having witnessed the passing away of the
Roman empire within which she had her birth, took
her place in the new English empire which was then
just starting on its great career. To grasp rightly the
main facts of this period is to understand the position
of London as a city of two empires.

When King Ælfred stood in London in the year 886

it is quite obvious that, decayed and neglected as the
city had become, it was a city with life in it, and it is
our present business to inquire what that life was.

There were the physical and monumental remains
of the Roman city.   Let us note, then, the remains of
Roman-built residences.   There is first of all to note
the recently discovered bath in Cannon Street, showing
all the usual features, and other remains at Austin
Friars.   But the principal remains are pavements discovered in modern times twelve or fifteen feet below
the existing level of no less than fifty-six streets.
I will enumerate the sites where these pavements have
been found, and I think in the end it will be agreed that
it is worth while to have considered such a list.[1]

Bank of England   A red, black and grey pavement
    under the south-west angle of the building and
    several others covering the area between Princes
    Street, Lothbury, and Bartholomew Lane
Birchin Lane.   Fragments of pavements of different
    colours.
Bishopsgate.   Three pavements, one of black and white
    tesserae in squares and diamonds.
Broad Street.   Three pavements. one forming the floor
    of a room 28 feet square.
Bucklersbury.   A magnificent pavement in colours.
Bush Lane.   Two pavements of white tesserae.
Camomile Street.   An undescribed pavement.
Cannon Street   Two pavements, one of red tesserae.
Cheapside.   An undescribed pavement.
Clement's Lane.   Fragments of pavements.
Cloak Lane.   A pavement of the herring-bone type.
College Street, Dowgate Hill.   Fragments of pave-
    ments.

[1] This list is compiled from the *Victoria History of London*.

ROMAN PAVEMENT DISCOVERED IN LEADENHALL STREET.

Crosby Square, Bishopsgate. Pavement of white and grey tesserae.

Crutched Friars. Undescribed pavement.

Dowgate Hill Fragments of pavements.

Fenchurch Street Three pavements, one of red, grey, and white tesserae, one of red tesserae only, one of richly coloured design on white ground.

Finch Lane. Part of a pavement of red, white black, and green tesserae, and fragments of other pavements

Friday Street Fragment of coarse tessellated pavement.

Gracechurch Street. Fragments of several pavements, and one pavement of considerable extent.

Gresham Street. Fragments of several pavements of white mosaic.

Grocers' Hall, Princes Street. Pavement of concrete

Guildhall. Pavement of grey slate and white marble.

Holborn (Viaduct end). Pavement of black, red, and white tesserae.

Honey Lane Pavement of red and yellow tesserae.

Huggin Lane, Wood Street. Fragments of pavement of white tesserae

King's Arms Yard, Moorgate Street. Fragments of pavement of red, white, and grey tesserae

Lambeth Hill. Fragment of pavement undescribed

Laurence Pountney Lane A large space covered by pavement of coarse red tesserae.

Leadenhall Market A beautiful pavement.

Leadenhall Street. A pavement, forming the floor of a room more than 20 feet square, of a Bacchus design, a room paved with red tesserae; another pavement undescribed and two fragments.

Lombard Street. Considerable remains of a pavement of coarse red tesserae; pavements all along the length of the street down to Birchin Lane, as if for a series of houses, and two other pavements

Lothbury. Remains of tessellated pavement.

Mansion House. Pavement now in Guildhall.

Mark Lane. Pavement of common red tesserae.

ROMAN STATUARY. DEAE MATRES.

Monument Street.   Fragment of pavement with a zigzag border and inscription.

Northumberland Alley, Crutched Friars.   Fragment of tessellated pavement.

Pancras Lane.   Small pieces of pavement.

Paternoster Row.   A pavement extending to 40 feet, with birds and beasts in compartments: part of another pavement of similar pattern.

Paternoster Square.   Fragment of plain pavement.

Poultry.   Part of a pavement.

Queen Street.   A pavement 14 feet square.

Little St. Helens   Undescribed pavement of tesserae.

St. Mary Axe.   Tessellated pavement undescribed.

St. Mary le Bow, Cheapside.   Pavement undescribed.

St Michael. Crooked Lane.   Plain red tessellated pavement.

St Olave, Jewry.   Pavement of red tesserae measuring 20 feet by 3 feet.

St. Paul's.   Tessellated pavement of a variegated pattern of rosettes on white ground.

St. Thomas Apostle.   Pavement of red, white, yellow, and black tesserae.

Seething Lane.   Pavements throughout the street.

Size Lane, Budge Row.   Pavement undescribed.

Suffolk Lane.   Pavement undescribed.

Thames Street, Lower.   Pavement of red and yellow tesserae, a second pavement connected with extensive remains of buildings.

Thames Street, Upper.   Fragments of pavements.

Threadneedle Street   Coarse red tessellated pavement 6 feet by 5 feet of white and black tesserae; fragments of similar pavements; another pavement 13½ feet long in variegated tesserae, and a third pavement.

Tower Hill.   Red tessellated pavement.

Wood Street.   Pavements of tesserae.

Now this long catalogue of pavements is evidence of the existence of a considerable mass of Roman

public and domestic remains in modern times, and
therefore also in Anglo-Saxon times. Most of them
are found connected with walls and other fragments
of buildings, and one or two of them with extensive
remains, sufficient to indicate their importance,
notably that on the site of the Coal Exchange,
and that in Bucklersbury. The latter gives us an
interesting picture, with just the required touch to
make it surrender to our imagination a glimpse of the
actual life that was lived there. There was a small
pavement entire, and beneath it the flues for heating
the apartment, while portions of the house to which it
belonged were also found stretching away to the bank
of the Walbrook, with the remains of a verandah on the
front overlooking the stream. One would not have
missed this record of the verandah for a bucket-full
of unemotional discoveries.

If we can discover this telling remnant of Roman
London, King Ælfred must have seen it undestroyed
Indeed this is the point I am anxious to press.
A verandah remaining for us to discover was a thing
of reality when Ælfred was king—perhaps a still-
frequented part of a house then inhabited by the
commercial successors of the Roman builder. These
remains are too numerous, too impressive in their
destroyed condition, for them to have been simply
ruins of a former grandeur when King Ælfred in
A.D. 886, more than one thousand years ago, surveyed
the great city, and took stock of its position for the
purposes of state government

Such remains were not ruins always. They were
Roman buildings and in them I doubt not lived the
men who brought London through the stress and trouble

of conquest, unconquered and undestroyed. We may
then turn from the buildings to the men, or rather
to the work of the men, for of the men themselves
we know nothing.

The houses were the shell within which the domestic
life was centred, and this indicates a domestic life of
the Roman type. No mere tribal-governed Celt or
Saxon lived in the square rooms, heated by the elaborate
hypocaust system, paved with tesserae of elaborate and
cultured designs, and occupying all the best parts of
the city. Living in Roman houses, Londoners lived in
Roman fashion and were governed by Roman organization and institutions. The forum discovered beneath
the site of modern Leadenhall Market, the mint on
the same site as at the present day, indicated by a silver
ingot inscribed as 'from the workshop of Honorius' discovered at the Tower in association with unworn coins
of Honorius,[1] the temple to Diana discovered beneath
St Paul's Cathedral, quays, walls, and foundations everywhere, indicate a solid civilization coming from a great
past. King Ælfred saw all these things and took stock
of them. Standing at any one of the city gates,
he would grasp the fact, perhaps too the significance,
of the unbuilt belt of land all round the city, the
sacred pomerium; he would be informed of the rights
of the citizens over a vast stretch of territory now
forming modern Middlesex on the north, and stretching
to Crayford and Wimbledon on the south, rights which
were actually recorded in the Anglo-Saxon Chronicle
when in A D. 912, his son, King Eadward, took possession of London, 'and of all the lands which belonged

thereto'; he would learn that the city had its own
commercial law derived from the Roman institutes;
its own criminal and personal law, which even preserved the criminal jurisdiction of the consul one mile
outside the city at our Mile End; its own property
law, derived directly from the Roman institutes,
its own school of trained lawyers faithfully carrying
out the customs of ancient Rome herself as Horace
describes them; its own governing authority constituted of a recognized governing class of citizens—
in a word, he saw a Roman city in the midst of his
Anglo-Saxon tribalism. The great king. I say, must
have seen all this and much more, for amidst the
details of city life and custom which have survived in
the later records and by tradition, all these points
have been preserved. He saw, and what is more, he
understood.

It is from the legal and constitutional side that the
most important evidence is derived, and it is fortunate
that this is so. It is not only more permanent in its
results, it is more definite in its application, and cannot
be got rid of by mere argument.

There was first of all, a whole body of merchant law.
Laws do not concern themselves with merchants and
merchandise until civilization has well advanced, and
then it becomes necessary to define what merchants
may do and may not do. We find none of these laws
among the tribal codes of the Celts of Ireland and
Wales, nor among those of the Anglo-Saxons. We find
London governing herself by such laws, and carrying on
the principles of Roman commercial law late down in
mediaeval days. Thus, under Roman law she made
commercial agreements with other cities to carry on

trade with safety and mutual benefit; under later
custom, incorporated in royal charters, she followed
exactly the same practice. ' Let one measure and one
weight pass such as is observed at London and at
Winchester' is the significant wording of a law of
King Eadgar, showing the country at large to have
been governed by a different law from that of these
two cities. In this case the London law was to become
the law of the country. In another important instance
London law had to be altered to meet the social conditions of the country. Under Celtic and Anglo-Saxon
laws the kindred to which the individual belonged
was the body answerable for all legal actions instead
of the individual. And, therefore, when we find London
in Athelstan's days passing a new law for itself and
obtaining the king's sanction thereto in order to make
it current law throughout the kingdom a new law which
provided for the formation of artificial groups of men in
commercial London to cope with the kinship groups in
Anglo-Saxon and Celtic Britain, it is clear that the
importance of this law is not indicated so much by its
terms as by the fact that it was newly made in Anglo-
Saxon times, and that up to that time at all events
a different law altogether had obtained. This other law
could only have been the Roman law of individual respon-
sibility. Again, under Roman law property could only
be devised upon one plan : one-third to the wife, one-
third to the children, and one-third as the testator willed,
and this was London law, and London law only, until
it was abolished by statute in the reign of George I.
And this is in direct contrast to the tribal law of the
Anglo-Saxons which obtained all round London, by
which the youngest son inherited the family home-

stead, and from which special custom the well-known London place-name of ' Kentish Town' is derived.

No one can doubt the importance of these facts They are governing factors in the life of the city, not merely surviving customs of comparatively little importance.   They reveal the constitution of the city, and the origin of that constitution from its Roman organization.   The addition to such legal customs of importance of customs of lesser importance to citizen life, but of equal weight as to origin, helps us to understand the general succession of Roman organization in London after Roman London had ceased to be.   Foremost among these customs is the group of rights and ceremonial observances showing London's control of the territory outside its own area—a weakened and weakening control, but a control which takes us back to the pomerium and the territorium for the only possible sources of their origin.   The belt of land outside the city walls included in the city area, and now known as wards ' without', must have been derived from an ancient condition of things long prior to the necessities of a walled city   The covering in of the fosse and the use of the land thus acquired will not account for the extent of the wards of Bishopsgate Without, Cripplegate Without and Farringdon Without, and this extent of territory, unaccounted for in mediaeval records, can be explained by the position of the Roman pomerium, encroached upon from without as the Anglo-Saxons worked their way towards London.   Beyond this narrow belt of land round the city there was the extended area within which the city had remarkable rights—the jurisdiction of the Sheriff of London over all Middlesex, the right of the citizens to hunt up as far as the Chilterns and in Middlesex and Surrey, and curious ceremonies and rites which have always given the city a position in outer London which its municipal constitution as derived from mediaeval sources never gave it.

I next come to a more important fact. Christianity in becoming the formal religion of the Roman empire had adopted from the first the methods of Roman civilization. Let me note the fact of Christian churches being built upon the walls of Roman cities. There are several such in London There are All Hallows on the Wall, the vestry of which is built out of the bastion, and St. James on the Wall, and there was St. Augustine on the Wall, now destroyed. A further fact of importance to note is that Christian churches were built on Roman sites and were probably Roman buildings themselves. St Martin's at Canterbury is a Roman building, and so is St. Michael's at Verulam. The foundations of the church of St. Andrew Hubbard. which stood on the south side of Little Eastcheap, had all the character of Roman workmanship (*Gent Mag Lib.* 193) and the same may be said of the unique remains of St. Michael's, Crooked Lane, and St. Gabriel. Fenchurch Street (*ibid* 211). Even St. Saviour's Southwark. and Westminster Abbey are now known to have been built upon Roman sites. This is evidence of material continuity — the continuity of Roman buildings used for Christian worship, withstanding the destruction which swept over the land at the time of the Saxon invasion. It helps towards the conception of a continuity in other directions. When our kings of the eighth century set their hands to documents written in Latin and bristling with the technical terms of the Roman law, whence do they obtain the knowledge? Certainly not from themselves. All the earliest charters are of ecclesiastical origin, all of them convey the absolute ownership of lands to the Church. The recorded motive which prompts a king to set his cross, for there is no signature, to a charter is a purely personal motive. He wishes to save his soul, he desires pardon for his crimes Of the religion of his realm he says not a word; it is his soul which must be saved, not his kingdom which must be benefited. He is acting therefore as a private landowner might act, and he uses terms and phrases which belong to the private law of Rome (Maitland, *Domesday Book*, 230). He uses terms and phrases unknown to his native Saxon law, unknown, I think we may say, to himself, perhaps not understood by himself, and he uses these terms and phrases at the instance of his ecclesiastical advisers, who in planting the Christian Church in Roman Britain made it a great territorial institution by means of Roman law, whose technical terms conveyed more meaning, much more meaning, into the species of ownership transferred to the Church than those who granted it ever understood.

We have thus tried to find out the kind of London which King Ælfred visited and restored to its place as an institution of the state, and I want now to point the principal interest of this for us. It marks the period of transfer from a Roman imperial city to an English imperial city King Ælfred was at the parting of the ways. It was his strong hand which moved the Anglo-Saxon conception of the state sufficiently forward to bring within its sphere of influence and activity the

institution of the city. The city which thus found
itself at the beginning of a new empire was of Roman
origin. It had belonged to one great imperial system,
and it was now going to take its place in another great
imperial system We of this age look back upon the
events which make of London a doubly imperial city
with the satisfaction of a happily completed task.
We cannot, if we would, understand all the struggles,
or the strength of the human effort, which made the
thing possible—those struggles which have left scars
upon the great city even to this day What we can
do is to estimate rightly the facts of history and
archaeology which belong to this period. This estimate reveals a city with a domestic life and culture,
with a legal system, with a governing constitution
entirely at variance with the Anglo-Saxon polity and
entirely in keeping with the Roman polity Anglo-
Saxon kings had ignored London, and London had
carried on her existence in a sort of constitutional
independence—an independence not granted to her as
a matter of state policy, but created by her as a means
of existence. Ælfred broke into that independence by
bringing London into definite relationship with English national life, and in the succeeding centuries we
have evidence of the remoulding of London citizen-
life more in accord with English ideas.

CHAPTER VIII

THE SAXONS IN LONDON

IF my reading of the evidence is correct, the Anglo-Saxons entered London, controlled it, mastered it, but they did not conquer it. They did not sail up the Thames, as they did the Severn and the Tyne and the lesser rivers. They entered England by the back door, as Dr Ripley says, and spread inland from the southern coast, prevented from following up the Thames by the presence of London.[1] We find them settling all round London in places which can be recognized by their terminals -ham, -ington, -ey, and -wich. That this settlement took place before they occupied London is proved by one very significant fact, namely, that the communal institutions of the Saxons, represented in later history by the manor, while existing all round the city, right up to its very boundary lines, never got into the city. There is evidence here, also, that something opposed to the village system of the Anglo-Saxons must have stood up against that system, to have prevented its entry within the city bounds. The city constitution, withstanding the village institutions of the Anglo-Saxon intruders, was a living thing therefore—a constitution under which men lived and, if

---

[1] *Races of Europe*, 323.

need were, fought, and in this case fought successfully.

The entry, control, and mastering of London by the
Anglo-Saxons therefore was not by conquest. History
is silent on the point, and the silence is eloquent, not
of fighting and conquest, but of a gradual encroachment
upon the city territorium, the gradual filling in with
villages and land-settlements of a territory which
previously had none such.

The silence of history as regards the London of Anglo-
Saxon times is only effectively broken when the country was exposed to the deadliest danger from outside.
The Danes and Northerners had included England in
their sphere of activity, and at once the importance of
London as a military defence post was discovered,
as we have seen, by the greatest of Anglo-Saxon kings
He repaired the walls and took ample measures for its
defence, says the Anglo-Saxon Chronicle. And London
held its own during the long struggle. 'Oft they
fought against the city of London, but praise be to
God that it stands sound, and they there ever met
with ill fare,' is the evidently contemporary record of
the year 1009. The same evidence comes from Danish
sources, as we learn from Saxo Grammaticus. Frode is
described as attacking London, 'the most populous
city of the island, but the strength of its walls gave
him no chance of capturing it,' and so he resorted
to treachery.[1] London stood sound always She accepted the Danish monarchy only when all England
had perforce accepted it. And the actual facts of the
Danish conquest appear to me to represent what must
have been a very close parallel to the facts of the

earlier Anglo-Saxon conquest, which cannot be recovered from history.

Let us look at the Danish events, as they concern London, a little closely. The Danes were kept outside London long enough for them to establish settlements there.   Everywhere else they settled within the cities they overwhelmed.   At Rochester they settled inside the city   At Dublin they did the same.   We discover evidences of the same kind of settlement at London as at Dublin and Rochester, strangely, remarkably alike, but it is outside the city boundaries, not inside.   We have first the important settlement of St. Olave in Southwark, and secondly the settlement of Aldwych on the western side of London, in Middlesex.   Of the former there does not appear to be any remains except the one important fact of its Scandinavian name and the dedication of its church.   Of the latter there are very significant remains

I will indicate what these remains are.   Colonel Prideaux, a well-known London antiquary, thus describes the territory —

South of Great Queen Street is a district which was coextensive with the area which was perhaps the oldest suburb of London, the village of Ealdwic or Aldwic, known later as Aldewych, and of which so late as the days of the Stuarts some vestiges remained in Oldwich Close, an open space which lay to the south of Lincoln's Inn Fields.   This village in the tenth century was largely colonized by the Danes, after whom the neighbouring church of St. Clement was named.   The highroad of the village, which connected it with the hospital of St. Giles, was known as the Via de Aldewych, and is represented by the modern Drury Lane, with the

exception of the south-eastern extremity which led to
the holy well of St Clement, and the name of which
still survives in Wych Street.—*Notes and Queries*, 9th
ser., ii 81.

This is the territory which I think was Danish
territory in the tenth century, and which was sufficiently separate from the City and from Westminster
to have been excluded from both these places up to
the time of the reign of Edward the First.

So much for the territorial portion of the history ;
we can now turn to the constitutional history, for in
this, I think, we have many important clues not
hitherto properly brought into the history of London.
If, in connexion with a territory which kept its dis-
tinctiveness down to historical times, we can discover
customs which can only be explained by reference to
Danish customs in other places, the argument becomes
all the stronger that this must have been the place of
settlement of the Danish conquerors of the country
round London.

The most significant relic of this Danish settlement is the stone monolith at which the chief of the
tribe was installed and the assembly of the tribe met
to discuss and settle the affairs of the community.
This is to be identified with a stone cross, as it was
called in later days, which stood opposite the Bishop of
Worcester's house, now Somerset House, in the Strand,
and the means of identification are most interesting. In
the first place it was the spot where the manorial dues of
later days were paid This appears from a manor custom
first recorded, according to Hazlitt's *Tenures of Land*,
in the reign of Edward the First, whence it appears that
the dues for a piece of land in the parish of St Clement

Danes were six horseshoes paid annually · at the Stone Cross (*ad crucem lapidem*). This land passed into the possession of the Corporation of London, who still render annually six horseshoes for it at the Court of Exchequer. The important point here is that the manor dues were rendered at the stone cross—the dues of the community, that is. rendered at the place of assembly of the community. That this is a correct interpretation of the manor custom is to be gathered from further customs connected with this stone cross, so called. Thus. in the reign of Edward the First, 'the justices itinerant set at the stone cross' in the open air. The custom is alluded to by several authorities, and there can be no doubt that it occurred. An open air court of this kind just outside the walls of the city within which were halls and courts for the meeting of citizens is obviously of archaic significance. The justices came to it as to a place independent of the city or of Middlesex, and they came in conformity to ancient custom, not to thirteenth-century requirements. That ancient custom again takes us back to the Danish settlement where the heads of the tribe met, in London, as they did at Dublin and at Rochester, at a monolith or other significant landmark, and as, according to all ancient authorities, was the practice in Danesland and throughout Scandinavia. Every tittle of evidence therefore points to this stone in the Strand as the ancient meeting-place of the assembly of the Danish community. the place where they administered their affairs and their laws, surviving in later days, before the district had lost its ancient idiosyncrasy of independence of both London and Westminster, to be administered by the King's justices but in the

archaic Danish fashion and in the ancient Danish spot [1]

There is the additional significance of the Maypole of the Strand, so well known as connected with this spot. It was placed a door or two westward beyond 'where Catherine Street descends into the Strand'.[2] The Maypole and its accompanying ceremonial is a very ancient relic of the past, and it is essentially connected with a settled community. Nowhere in England is it otherwise than a public institution, a part of the corporate life of the people. On the continent of Europe it is something more than this—it is connected with the special feature of early life, namely, the tribal community, and above all the tribal community of the Northmen. That it should have survived so strongly in this particular spot in London justifies the assumption that it comes down from the same tribal community of the Danes, who settled outside London walls, and gave the name of Aldwych to this district. Indeed, there is a curious passage in William of Malmesbury about the election of Harold, son of Canute, in 1036, which I think illustrates the point at which we have arrived. Harold, we are told, was elected by the Danes and the citizens of London, 'who from long intercourse with these barbarians had almost entirely adopted their customs'. There is no evidence of these customs having obtained within the city, and

[1] Hazlitt, *Tenures of Land*, 203 ; Ritson, *Court Leets*, ix ; *Chronicle of the Mayors and Sheriffs of London*, 237, 243 ; Pennant, *London*, 159 , Stow's *Survey* (edit Kingsford), ii 93

[2] Hone's *Everyday Book*, i. 280, gives a good account from a scarce tract of 1661 of the re-erection of this Maypole after the Restoration, and Virtue's engraving of the procession of both Houses of Parliament to St Paul's Cathedral after the Peace of Utrecht, July 7, 1713, contains a glimpse of it as it then stood

I suggest we have here a record of what was happening just outside London.

Here, then, we have the chief features of the Danish settlement in London. The Danes settled in their own fashion, not in English fashion or in London fashion. Their settlement was outside London, not within it. They lived under their own institutions. The laws of the tenth century constantly refer to the Danes living under laws of their own, and though I do not necessarily connect this with a Danelagh territory—the laws were tribal, not territorial—they undoubtedly obtained in all Danish settlements.

Now the interest of this survival from the past history of Danish influence in London is twofold. First, it shows a singularly powerful London capable of holding its own against the mightiest foes the English ever encountered. Secondly, it shows by analogy that what the Danes did in the eleventh century—were obliged to do because of the vigorous capacity of London to defend itself—is what the Anglo-Saxons might well have done in the seventh and succeeding centuries. They settled all round London—in their Kensingtons, Paddingtons, Fulhams, Lewishams, and the like, just as the Danes settled immediately outside London in their fewer numbers. History repeated itself. The great city had an organization capable of being used for defensive purposes. That it was used against the Danes most effectively, we have historical and archaeological evidence. That it was similarly used against the Anglo-Saxons is what all the evidence permits, and the parallel seems to me to be conclusive.[1]

[1] Freeman, Hist. Norman Conquest, i. 43-5, draws attention to the many par...

The organization which enabled the citizens of London so to act, must have been of a high order. We get no evidence of such organization from the Saxon side. All that the Saxon evidence shows is neglect of London. Until the Danes entered into conflict with the Saxons, the position of London as an important military centre was entirely overlooked No Saxon monarch had ever used it as a basis of military operations, and so far as the evidence goes London was left to itself. The organization, therefore, which allowed it to defend itself against the Danes, must have been other than Anglo-Saxon, and the only possible source for such an organization must have been the old Roman system kept up through these years of neglect.

When, however, the London of the eleventh century was defending itself against the Danes, it was doing so under an Anglo-Saxon king, under an Anglo-Saxon domination therefore. We should expect, then, to find Anglo-Saxon influences and institutions in London, even if they do not appear as the only influences and institutions. This is in point of fact what is to be found. We see one group of customs taking its place clearly and distinctly as municipal law, and another group of customs delegated to the position of municipal usage only, having no force as municipal law. Municipal law may be traced back to Roman origins. Municipal usage is Anglo-Saxon. It never dominates the city It invigorates it. It asserts itself in an obstinate sort of fashion—the very assertion making its place as a secondary influence all the more pronounced.

I can illustrate this view by one interesting example —the position of the sword in the municipal ceremonial of London. A copy of a letter exists among the archives of London, dated about 1582, written by the Lord Mayor to the Lord Chancellor, and complaining 'that when he (the Lord Mayor) attended to take his oath without the Tower Gate, he had Her Majesty's sword carried before him in the streets, as had been the custom to carry it in Westminster Hall until they came to the bar of Her Majesty's Court, when the sword was reversed by the sword-bearer as in the presence of Her Majesty; and so it had intended to be done when arriving at the place where the Lieutenant sat as had been the custom. They were met at the corner of Tower Street by two of the warders, who commanded Her Majesty's sword to be holden down, and pressed violently to take it down, but through the good discretion of the Recorder they were peaceably holden off'.[1] And later on, in 1633, a similar dispute took place with reference to the right of the Lord Mayor to have the sword borne up before him within St. Paul's Cathedral, and 'especially within the choir'.[2] Now this right, thus tenaciously defended in the sixteenth and seventeenth centuries, according to ancient custom, carries us farther back into antiquity than the date of the dispute. That this view of the case is the correct one is proved by the curious analogy which exists in a self-governing community whose origin and practice is admittedly archaic. One of the ceremonies incidental to the great folk-meeting on Tynwald Hill, in the Isle of Man, was according 'to the constitution of old time', that the lord should 'sitt in a chaire . . with the sword before him holden with the point upwards'.[3]

[1] Remembrancia, p 432. [2] Ibid, 328.
[3] Train Hist of Isle of Man ii 188

It should not be forgotten that here we have a typical
ceremony of the election of the tribal chiefs of primitive communities, and the parallel to municipal custom
is not too far apart to indulge in the conclusion that
in this example of old municipal custom we have a
survival from old tribal custom.

The folkmoot of London illustrates this position in
a still more remarkable manner. We can not only see
it at the time of its decay, but we can see it in all its
primitive condition from the records of its later doings
In an institution of this kind late records are as good as
early. They follow traditional practices and forms,
they keep up rights and privileges, they follow ancient
rites and ceremonies. The very name of the institution,
the folkmoot of London, invites attention. No other
city possesses such a title for its assembly. It is pure
Saxon enshrining the Saxon ideal of self-government
There were three chief folkmoots during the year.
'At the Michaelmas folkmoot the meeting gathers to
know who is the sheriff and to hear the new sheriff's
charge. The Christmas meeting is for keeping the
wards or arranging for their watch. The third, at
Midsummer. is to keep the city from fire on account of
the great drought.' The London interpolator of the
laws of Edward the Confessor, says Miss Bateson,
ordered that the wards should be arranged and careful
provision made against fire in the folkmoot. Later
on, these duties of watch and protection against fire
devolve upon the wardmoots, but whilst there is but
one sheriff the folkmoot appears as still an administrative body of some importance.

'Any Londoner who neglects these folkmoots is in
the king's forfeiture for 10s. But by the law of

London the sheriff ought to cause inquiry to be made concerning any of whom he would know whether he is present. If there be any one who is asked for and not there he ought to be summoned to the husting and be brought thither by the law of the city. If the good man says that he was not summoned that is to be known by the beadle of the ward If the beadle says he was summoned at the husting he shall be attainted thereof, for the beadle has no other witness nor ought to have but the great bell which is rung for the folkmoot at St. Paul s.' [1]

This ringing of the great bell of the cathedral church to summon the people to their folkmoot is singularly indicative of the democratic character of the assembly. No picking and choosing, not even a voting for representative members, but a gathering of every citizen— a mass meeting assembled in formal fashion to accomplish constitutional business. It met in the open air upon a piece of ground at the east end of St. Paul's Church adjoining the cross,[2] and in the struggles it had with the selected body of citizens who claimed the right of governing the city it used the ancient formulae in giving its decisions, formulae which are represented wherever a primitive example of the Teutonic folkmoot has been preserved on the Continent, in Switzerland, Prussia, Denmark, and Scandinavia— it pronounced its 'Yea, Yea', or 'Nay, Nay', and the business was ended.

We always find the London folkmoot struggling for its existence, struggling against a more limited organi-

---

[1] *Liber Albus*, 118-19, Miss Bateson, *Eng. Hist. Rev.*, xvii. 502

[2] *Liber Custumarum*, 338-9, and see my early work on *Primitive Folkmoots*, 158

zation which held the real power. This struggle is the key-note to its history. It never possessed full control of the city. It never was the governing assembly. It had got into the city with its English citizens, but it never reigned supreme. There was always up against it a superior limited authority. a high class of citizens, optimates, meliores. primates, potentates, and the two governing authorities represent the dual element in London after the Anglo-Saxon authority had entered the city. The citizens in folkmoot called themselves 'the commons of the city', and they fought against 'the discreet men of the city' on several memorable occasions. They had finally to fight against more redoubtable enemies, namely the Chapter of St. Paul's Cathedral, among whose papers is preserved the record of the enclosure of the piece of land on which the mayor and commonalty used to hold their court which is called Folkmoot' and the protest of the citizens before the justices at the Tower.[1] This last act took place in the fourteenth year of King Edward II, and we do not hear of the folkmoot after that date. It had had a fitful and struggling history It went down before the more powerful authority which the city, on every occasion when events are revealed by a constitutional struggle, always put into force and which always seemed to win the fight

I think the final history of the folkmoot of London may be traced, following out the process of evolution apparent in all English institutions. The husting is an integral part of the folkmoot, perhaps it is the folkmoot. Mr Maitland will have it that the

---

1 Historical MSS. Commission iv 49

husting is a house thing, as distinct from a thing
or court held in the open air.[1] The open-air
meeting of the London folkmoot continued down
to the thirteenth century, and it is somewhat difficult to trace out its connexion with the husting
if Mr. Maitland's definition is correct. I venture to
suggest, however, that it is not I think it is the
thing formed by the housemen of the community, the
men who owned a homestead, the full members of the
ancient tribal organization, and Icelandic law should
tell us this much.[2] That the folkmoot became divided
into two as events marched on is the way I read the
evidence. Administratively it passed into the common
hall, juridically it passed into the husting This kind
of change seems to be apparent throughout the entire
history of the primitive assembly as it passed into the
local court As Sir Henry Maine puts it of the
Manorial Court, 'three courts are usually included
which legal theory keeps apart, the Court Leet, the
Court Baron, and the Customary Court of the Manor'.
I think there cannot be reasonable doubt of the
legitimate descent of all three from the assembly of
the township,'[3] so I would put it of the folkmoot in relationship to the Court of Husting and Common Hall,
there cannot be reasonable doubt of their descent from
the folkmoot.

I think it will be interesting to make a note of the

---

[1] *Domesday Book and Beyond*, 211 This is the Bosworth and Toller
definition in *Anglo-Saxon Dictionary*, s v , but there is no authority given,
while for the hustings court meeting in the open air see Mildmay's
Elections of London, edited by Causton, p cxxvii

[2] See the glossary to Morris's *Saga Library*, vi 161-6.

[3] Maine, *Village Communities*, 139, and cf. Maitland, *Select Pleas of
Manorial Courts*, pp xvi xix.

last sitting of the Court of Husting   It is reported in the *Times*, March 13, 1901 · 'A sitting of the Court of Hustings, the first which has taken place for some years, was held at the Guildhall yesterday afternoon. The Lord Mayor, who was attended by the sword and mace bearers and the City Marshal, presided, and there were also present Mr. Alderman and Sheriff Vaughan Morgan, the Recorder, the Town Clerk, and other high officers of the Corporation.   There is a Court of Hustings of Pleas of Land, and a Court of Hustings of Common Pleas, and they are now held only when business requires.   The Lord Mayor, Aldermen, and Sheriffs are the Judges, and the Recorder sits with them to pronounce the judgements of the Court.   The City Solicitor (Sir H. H. Crawford), addressing the Court, said that the sitting was held for the enrolment of two deeds   One of the deeds was dated January 15, 1897, the other July 4, 1899.   The Court directed the deeds to be enrolled   There being no other business to be disposed of, the sitting of the Court was adjourned.'

There is one additional fact of remarkable significance which helps to prove that London in Anglo-Saxon times was of little importance until its military position was recognized by Ælfred, and it was used as a defence against the Danes.   This fact is the character of the Anglo-Saxon objects which have been found from time to time during excavations.   Only two of these objects can be identified as belonging to a period earlier than the Danish invasion—one is a buckle of beautiful workmanship of the fifth century, and the other a bronze brooch of cruciform type, found in Tower Street, in 1868, and belonging to the fifth or early sixth

century All the rest of the Anglo-Saxon finds belong
to the Danish period, and consist largely of swords,
spear-heads, and other weapons—just that class of objects
which fits in well with the other evidence, to show that
London was not an Anglo-Saxon city until it became
the battle-ground against Danish encroachment. The
Victoria History of London has gathered together and
illustrated this part of the subject in a remarkably able
way, and it is impossible to resist the argument which
it adds to what from historical sources appears so
clear

There is, however, a still more notable fact, namely,
the absence of Saxon burials in London, in direct contrast to numerous grave finds of the West-Saxon type,
which extend from Kent to as far north as the Humber,
though avoiding London. The Celts of London, as we
have seen, were buried there as they had lived there,
and the avoidance of London as a burial-place for the
dominant English is explainable only if it were not
also a living place. This not only accords with London's
position of quasi-independence of Anglo-Saxon occupation, but it nowhere finds a solution if we consider
it by any of the conclusions of historians as to the
Anglo-Saxon treatment of London. The avoidance
of London as a burial-place means the avoidance of it
as a homing-place, even the avoidance of it as a battle-
ground The English before Ælfred cared not for the
great city and left it to its languishing commerce and
its restricted life. The great king brought it out
again as a city capable of doing great things for the
state.

The Saxons in London, therefore, were not Saxons of
London. They went there because of their supreme

necessity when a strategic position was an essential
feature of their defence against the northern foeman,
and they found not only a strategic position but a well-
organized government which could be reckoned upon
to exert its whole force in its own defence. The Saxon
put his hand on this living institution made it partly
conform to his own ideals but left intact all the
principal features which had brought it so powerfully
under Saxon rule.

CHAPTER IX

WHAT LONDON WAS TO THE SAXONS

LONDON meant nothing constitutionally to the Anglo-Saxons. Their kings were not crowned within its walls, but on king-stones, as at Kingston, fifteen miles from London, and as the evidence seems to point, at Thorney, just outside London. The evidence for Westminster being a place for the crowning of Anglo-Saxon kings depends upon a series of details which I have described in my *Governance of London* and therefore need not repeat here. But an additional argument is, I think, derived from Mr Lethaby's recent research into the architecture of Westminster Abbey,[1] which he thinks was designed for the ceremonial of the coronation. If this is so, the idea must have been derived from tradition and from custom existing at the time of Edward the Confessor, and this takes us to the institutions of the Saxons outside the city walls. Then, too, the meetings of their witenagemot were generally held at places in the country under the vault of heaven, and only two are recorded as taking place in London. one by Coenulf of Mercia in 811, who then called it 'that illustrious place and royal city' (*loco preclaro oppidoque regali*). and by Egbert of Wessex in 833. London did not fit in with Anglo-Saxon institutions.

It fitted in better with the Church's conception of

what the new nation should be. As Mr. Dale so well explains, 'the landing of Augustine appeared to Æthelbert of Kent to be an event of as great political as religious importance.' It meant a connexion with the great empire, and Mr. Dale thinks that under the influence thus fostered, ' London became a busy mart and flourishing port, keeping up continual intercourse with the merchants of Roman Gaul '.[1]

Everything we know of London in Anglo-Saxon times fits in with this conclusion, and it confirms its aloofness from the Anglo-Saxon constitution. At one time it was nominally included in the kingdom of the East Saxons, at another in that of the Kentishmen, at another in that of Mercia; but there are several facts of Anglo-Saxon history which go directly to show the real independence of the city. *East Saxoniam cum Lundonia* is the significant expression of Florence of the year 1016. The evidence of the coinage is perhaps the most significant of all. Coinage means commerce, and the sceattas struck in London during the Anglo-Saxon period have one great peculiarity. Quoting Mr. C. F. Keary, ' they alone among the coins of this series are of very base silver, sometimes indeed of a metal so debased that it becomes questionable whether they should not be described as copper coins Thus the metals of all the earliest English coins bearing the name of London are approximately very base silver or copper and gold, the metals of the two classes of Roman coins current in this country; a fact not without its significance, especially when we reflect that the preference for silver coins was in some sort a badge of the Teutonic nations. *Quantum valeat*, the circumstance tends to

1 N ̣   ̣ ̣ ̣   ̣ ̣ ̣

show that the city of London retained something of
the habits and preferences which it had acquired
under the Romans. At the same time the appearance
itself of the legend "Londonia" or "Londunium"
may suggest that during this period London preserved
some sort of autonomy.'[1] This evidence seems to
equate with all that has been previously adduced. Its
parallel is only to be found north of the Humber,
where the remains of Roman civilization are most
abundant In Kent, Surrey, and Essex there is nothing
like it, and once more we find London forming a centre
of its own in the midst of English surroundings.
Mr Freeman puts it thus: 'Among the shiftings of
the smaller English kingdoms London seems to have
held her own as a distinct power . . always keeping
somewhat of an independent being.[2]

It seems clear that this very well summarizes the
position. No English monarch ever granted it rights
and privileges. There is no constitutional document
which shows the city to owe any part of its constitution or its position to the favour or the prescience
of an English king The earliest mention of London
in Anglo-Saxon literature is a law of the seventh
century (Hlothhaere and Eadric) providing the method
by which a Kentishman might purchase chattels in
London—'let him have two or three true men to
witness or the king's wic-reeve'—which not only shows
the early commercial condition of London under Anglo-
Saxon rule, but the power to have a recognized proce-
dure in regard to outsiders who were not citizens The
great Ælfred s use of it as a strategical centre against

<hr />

[1] Keary, *Catalogue of English Coins in British Museum,* i xx

the Danish invader evidently points to an already existing organization, and the remarkable ordinance which 'the bishops and reeves belonging to London' ordained when Athelstan was king, shows, as we have already seen, that the law of the Londoners, from which this ordinance was a departure, did not belong to the Anglo-Saxon system of law. Even the grant by Athelstan of eight moneyers to London, more than to any other town, signifies the existence of a settled organization. We cannot be sure of the exact position London held under the Anglo-Saxons, but we can be sure that it was not a position of their making. It was a position carved out by London herself from her past position as a city of the Roman empire, and which helped her forward in later years, just such a position in point of fact as existed almost everywhere when Roman and barbarian met, as Ammianus Marcellinus describes the position of Strasburg. Brumat, Saverne, Spiers, Worms, and Mayence, which 'were all in the hands of the barbarians who were established in their suburbs, for the barbarians shunned fixing themselves in the towns themselves, looking upon them like graves surrounded with nets' (lib. xvi, cap ii).

This conclusion points to the possession of a city organization of some power and centralization. It cannot be that Bishop Stubbs is correct in his conclusion that when the city of London 'springs into historical light it is a collection of communities based on the lordship, the township, the parish, and the gild'.[1] There was only one community which passed the Athelstan ordinance, and there was only one community which sent forth its contribution to the

Saxon army at Hastings with its sheriff, Ansgar, at their head It was one community which received back the wounded Ansgar and parleyed with the great conqueror. London was everything to the Anglo-Saxons of the later period, but it was so much to them because it possessed a settled organization and a system of government 'Few pictures from the past', says Mr. Kemble, 'may the eye rest upon with greater pleasure than that of a Saxon portreeve looking down from his strong gyld-hall upon the well-watched walls and gates that guard the populous market of his city —Ealdredsgate et Cripplesgate, i e. *portas illas obser-vabant custodes* In the centre of the square stands the symbolic statue which marks the freedom of juris-diction and of commerce, balance in hand to show the right of unimpeded traffic. sword in hand to intimate the *ius gladii*, to show the right to judge and punish' [1]— a symbolism which came from the cities of the Roman empire.

Where, then, we may well ask, were the Saxons while London kept its more ancient Roman organiza-tion? Fortunately, the answer comes to us with great clearness from the Anglo-Saxon settlements all round the city. These settlements are unmistakable. They belong to a class existing practically all over the country, and finally in historical times developing into the manor. There are manors everywhere, as Mr. Seebohm puts it But the significant fact is that the manorial system does not penetrate into the city of London. It is at the very boundaries, but not beyond, and I will endeavour to show where this evidence is to be found.

[1] Kemble, Saxons Engl i 313

Anglo-Saxon London began, *not* within the walls of Lundinium, but without; not even at its gates, spreading outwards, but from outside, gradually approaching nearer and nearer. The new-comers settled all round, and we may trace out on the maps the records of the settlement. I have marked the sites of all the villages mentioned in Domesday within the present county of London, and one cannot but be struck with the significant position they occupy on the map.

There are two kinds of settlements: those up the river beyond the city influence, and those close to the city boundary. Those of the first class are the ancient settlements afterwards to grow into modern parishes —long, narrow territories stretching from the river to the hills. These settlements were arranged in English fashion, not Roman fashion. We see this by the maps. If we compare the manorial settlement round London with that of the more rural parts of the country— Wiltshire, for instance, would be an excellent example to refer to—we find them of exactly the same type. There is the homestead in the lowlands, near by are the meadow land and arable land, and stretching up towards the high lands are the open pastures and the forest. Examining some of these settlements a little more closely, let us consider the topography of modern Kensington, Fulham (with Hammersmith), Paddington, St Pancras, Islington, and the great manor of Stepney north of the Thames, and Lambeth and Camberwell south of the Thames. Each of these shows the same characteristic mode of settlement. north of the Thames they begin by the river, and stretch away from it northwards towards the heights; and again south of the Thames they begin at the river and stretch southwards towards the Surrey hills. Those of the second class are different. On the north there is the great territory south of the Roman road (now Oxford Street), known to us as Westminster, and stretching east and west along the river; and the Roman roadway represented by Edgware Road is the boundary between ancient manors and parishes represented by modern Paddington and Marylebone. On the south the ancient influences of Southwark interpose between the river and the normal manorial settlement.

There is, however, something more than the mere outline and fragments of such settlements. There are the traces of the internal system of economy. The village community system has been well examined in this country by Mr Seebohm, Mr. Slater, Sir Henry Maine, and some others, and one definite fact about it is the peculiar arrangement of the arable lands. No one owner possessed wide stretches of land, but each owner—each villager, I should say—held his acre strip side by side in definite rotation with other villagers, so that one holding of sixteen acre strips— the normal holding—was situated in sixteen different parts of the arable lands.

Now let me turn to the London evidence. First of all, I will introduce a word-picture from a chronicle narrative, the true explanation of which we owe to the scholarship and acumen of Mr Seebohm. Edward the Confessor lay dying at Westminster, and looking out on the scenery he loved so well—his contemporary biographer describes the palace as 'amongst fruitful fields lying round about it'—he saw in his delirium two holy monks, who foretold to him the coming disasters of the realm which should only be ended when 'the green tree, after severance from its trunk and removal for the space of three acres, should return to its parent stem and again bear leaf and fruit and flower'. Only one picture could have conjured up this otherwise unaccountable vision. The green tree was no doubt suggested by an actual tree, growing out of one of the balks separating the acre strips beyond Thorney island, and the uneven glass of the king's window-panes would be likely as he rose in his bed to sever the stem from its roots and transplant it higher up in the open field, in an acre strip three acres off, restoring it again to its root as he sank back upon his pillow. 'The very delirium of the dying king,' says Mr. Seebohm, 'thus becomes the most natural thing in the world when we know that all round were the open fields and balks and acres.'[1]

This word-picture, so cleverly extracted from the eleventh-century chronicle, appears in graphic form on the eighteenth-century maps of London, and its last relic survives in the name of 'Long Acre'. Because the acre strips have never been destroyed or altered, because year by year they have appeared in faithful surveys of London, the modern map becomes evidence of Anglo-Saxon London.

Scattered over the modern maps of London are examples of these acre strips. In the 'new' map of London, published in 1797, we have the acre strips shown particularly well in 'Battersea common-field', and at Lambeth, Fulham, Camberwell, and Peckham. In Horwood's map of 1794 the acre strips of Bermondsey are well marked, and in a map of Wandsworth manor of 1787, the distribution of the acre strips is

almost undisturbed. The common fields of Bayswater
are noted in *Notes and Queries*, vol i, p. 162

The alignments of some of our oldest roads help us
to understand this, as for instance the singular con-
formation of the frontage of houses at Putney—one or
two houses built up to a frontage line, and the next
one or two built a little in advance, and a third a little
further in advance, a fourth perhaps being a little
behind; the only possible interpretation of such peculiar
topographical features being that these were the terminals of the old acre strips upon which their owners
had built the modern villa and thus formed an irregular street front.

Perhaps, however, the most interesting example is
afforded by Park Lane. The glorious irregularity of
this most picturesque of thoroughfares was not due
to street architecture. All that street architects could
do is to be seen in the squares and streets at the
back of Park Lane. What they could not do was
to destroy the frontage line of the western boundary
of these estates Park Lane commences at the
Oxford Street end in almost a straight line, due. I
suggest to a late cutting of the road to form Hyde
Park, which took in a piece of the ancient continuation
of Edgware Road at this point. After this straight-
line commencement, terminating at about Wood's
Mews, it is wholly irregular, and irregular in a very
curious and interesting manner The houses from
Wood's Mews to Upper Brook Street are set back some
feet , after Upper Brook Street there is a further set
back up as far as the Mews, then a further setting back
of the houses to Upper Grosvenor Street ; after Mount
Street the same features appear, until the triangular

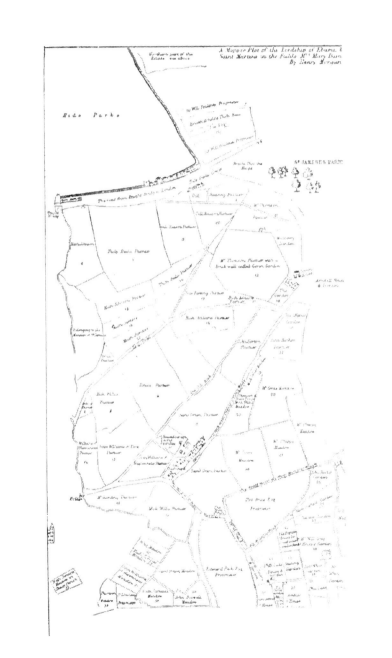

site of Dorchester House is reached. and beyond this
to Piccadilly the frontage line is never straight always
one length at the back of another length.

I always believed that this irregularity was of the
same nature as that at Putney already described,
namely, the terminal points of the various acre strips,
and proof of this is forthcoming if we turn to the
'mapp or plot of the Lordship of Eburie being situated
in the parish of Saint Martins in the Fields, Mary
Dammison being proprietress; by Henry Morgan,
1675,' in the Crace collection. At the top of the map
is 'the road from Knight Bridge to London', showing
incidentally the bridge over the dip in modern
Piccadilly, the site of the old stream of which the
Serpentine is still a relic The modern Park Lane is
drawn on the eastern side of Hyde Park, but the
eastern side of the road is not yet built upon Running
parallel to Piccadilly, and therefore at right angles to
Park Lane, are the acre strips with the names of the
owners recorded—

    (1) Sir William Poultney, proprietor
    (2) Brickhill Fields Thoby Beele.
    (3) Lee, Esq
    (4) [Unnamed.]
    (5) Sir William Poultney, proprietor.

Sir William Poultney is thus owner of two acre
strips separated by three other acre strips differently
owned. But this is not all. In a map of the Grosvenor
estate, dated 1723, Park Lane is shown built upon on
its eastern side from Oxford Street up to just beyond
Chapel Street, and 'Berkely Fields' remain unbuilt
upon, and show a triangular strip adjoining Park Lane,
as belonging to Mr Poultney This is exactly one of

those 'gores' of land so frequently found in unenclosed villages, and it is preserved to this day in the triangular site upon which Dorchester House now stands We have the name preserved to us in Kensington Gore. Thus, although we have not the whole distribution of the acre strips revealed by the maps, there is no question that these indications are sufficient to show the nature of the holdings of the entire area. They were acre strips belonging to the village community system. The terminals of the acre strips in modern Park Lane remained unaltered, and they account to us of to-day for the splendid irregularity of the building-line of this most fashionable of London streets, thus showing how the settlement system of the Anglo-Saxons has influenced the geography of modern London

It is, however, the geography of the area outside the city, not inside. Summing up at this point, I hope I have succeeded in showing Anglo-Saxon London with its homesteads in the fields in contradistinction to Roman London with its home life within city walls, with its institutions still in primitive form at Kingston, and only brought by the last Anglo-Saxon king into more civilized form at Westminster, with its commerce again forcing it into prominence and bringing Anglo-Saxon men into London citizenship—two separate Londons standing out in relief against each other in pre-Norman times. London within the walls being occupied no doubt by many English citizens, but not on that account departing from her more ancient life, communities of Englishmen outside the walls not caring for the great city.

CHAPTER X

THE LONDON TO WHICH THE NORMANS CAME

WITH the advent of the Normans London was no longer to be neglected—no longer to be used chiefly for its military strength. It was to be welded with the state, a part and parcel of the national government.

It is not quite impossible to picture the London which the Normans came to occupy. A walled town, with its gates and its defences, its cathedral church, and no doubt many of its ancient Roman buildings still standing, with its great market-place, or Cheapside, are what we may surmise with some certainty; and Mr. Kemble has drawn a picture which, coming from his hand, may be accepted in the main as true of London when the Normans came.[1]

Where we can add some extra details is the great bridge and the direction of the streets. The bridge meant much to London, not only to London's defence, but to her commerce. The twists in her streets are another matter. Underneath the streetway are found the remains of Roman pavements and other evidences of buildings on a different alignment from that of the present streets, and conclusions have been drawn from this that Anglo-Saxon London was built upon the

[1] *Saxons in England* ii. 310.

destroyed Roman city. It is not a conclusive argument. The rebuilding of the city after the successive
fires which have occurred there, and particularly after
the devastation of 1666, would account for many of
these cases; and if the Saxons here and there showed
their disregard of old landmarks, it cannot have been
very extensive. London was a living city, not a dead
collection of unused buildings, and during its four
centuries of life under Anglo-Saxon overlordship it
witnessed changes from fire, sieges, and other
catastrophes.

Apart from such conclusions as may be drawn from
the imperfect collection of pre-Norman facts, there is
something to be gained as a reflection from that
wonderful post-Norman description of the city drawn
up in the reign of King Henry II, great-grandson of the
Conqueror. The Normans had made changes, of course,
but changes only on the basis of what was already existing The cheery optimism of the Norman historian
leads him to show us a great London, not a new city;
to describe a steady life, not a newly imported system
taking the place of an older one destroyed : to reveal
citizens successful and happy in old ways and habits
inherited from long lines of ancestors and predecessors :
and if in some respects the city has been added to and
embellished by the Normans, it still retains the main
foundations of the older life Fitzstephen tells us of
St. Paul's Church, thirteen large conventual churches,
besides one hundred and thirty-six lesser parochial
ones. Besides the Tower, a Norman addition, he
describes two castles strongly fortified on the west
side, and walls high and thick, with seven double gates,
having on the north side towers placed at proper

intervals. The artisans of the several crafts, the
vendors of the various commodities, and the labourers
of every kind have each their separate station. The
city is divided into wards, and there are sewers and
aqueducts in its streets. It is governed by annual
sheriffs, an order of senators and inferior magistrates,
and on stated days it has its assemblies. The citizens
used the land outside the walls for garden ground and
pasturage, and schools, sports, and pleasures formed
an essential part of the life of London. The Normans
came to a city of renowned delight in the matter of
climate, commercial greatness, strength, and capacity
for development.

The system of government in London when the
Normans took it over, is an obscure but an important
point. So great an historian as Dr Stubbs can see
there nothing more than 'a bundle of communities,
townships, parishes, and lordships, of which each has
its own constitution', [1] and Dr. Round, who has examined so carefully the early administration of London
as it is revealed from the charters, endorses this view. [2]
Dr. Stubbs, to my mind, transferred to the earliest
Norman period some of the conditions of a later period,
the period before which London had regained its
communa. Dr. Round has in this instance followed
Dr. Stubbs instead of his own facts and critical faculty.
After his conclusive proof from the history of the
sheriff that London and Middlesex 'as far back as we
can trace them' are 'one and indivisible', he discusses
the character of the grant to the citizens of London of
the *corpus comitatus*, and concludes that 'the only
distinction between this lease and one to a private

---

[1] *Const. Hist.,* i. 404.   [2] *Geoffrey de Mandeville,* 356.

individual lies in the corporate character of the lessee'.
Exactly, but this 'only' difference is very important.
It cannot be that the lease would grant to an indeter-
minate body of citizens that which could only be
granted to a *corpus*. It cannot be that a *corpus* was
created incidentally in order to provide the machinery
for granting the lease. The *corpus* was in truth already
there. It may not have been in perfect form. The
remains of the Roman constitution had been eaten into
by the incoming Anglo-Saxon or Danish organization,
of which the folkmoot and the hustings are the representatives The result may not have produced an
entirely unified constitution. But a constitution of
some sort was there.

English London, then, to which the Normans came,
was a veritable city unit. It had material remains of
its Roman origin and also constitutional remains. It
had fragments from the newly awakened nationality
of the English, forced a little to the front by the
pressure of Danes and Northmen. It was such an
asset of national greatness as the Normans would turn
to full account. If it was a somewhat unformed city,
it possessed all the materials for future moulding at
the hands of the greatest statesmen of a great race.

CHAPTER XI

WHAT LONDON WAS TO THE NORMANS

LONDON meant everything constitutionally to the
Normans. They were determined to clothe their military success with their constitutional doctrine, and
few things are more interesting in national history
than the singularly effective manner with which the
Normans first of all drove right home their military
power and success, and then set up their constitutional
machinery to hide the ugliest of the results.

William's methods of approaching and dealing with
London illustrate this point   Direct conquest was not
his aim. It would have been attempted if need had
driven him to it, but he delayed even the attempt as
long as possible. And during the long period of delay
two things were happening. One was the cutting off
of London from the rest of the country by the inter-
position of the Norman army on its northern side after
it had devastated and laid waste the south. The other
was the opening and carrying on of negotiations with
the chiefs of the city. The superb brilliancy of the
whole transaction is what strikes the imagination of
the historian   But equally there is the extreme necessity for it all. The brilliancy of the double plans
belongs to William and his advisers. The necessity
for such careful handling belongs to the strength and
importance of London.

William's march upon London began at Hastings. He first went to Romney, taking 'what vengeance he would for the slaughter of his men' Thence to Dover and on to Canterbury and to Winchester From Winchester he marched along the old Roman road to Southwark and paused there awhile, first to beat back a sally from the city, secondly to give Southwark to the flames. Then he turned westward through Surrey, Hants, and Berks, crossing the Thames at Wallingford and wasting and subduing the lands all round London —the ancient *territorium* of Roman Lundinium—until he came to Berkhampstead in Herts.

There he opened negotiations. London had declared for Eadgar, grandson of the great Eadmund Ironside, but had found him wanting. He was no king to lead, to defend his country, to fight for And so William had his chance. He approached the great Sheriff Ansgar, who, wounded and sick from the field at Hastings, was still the centre of all the counsels taken by the defenders of London. The Chronicles tell us of messages passing between Ansgar and William, and at last one remarkable offer came from William that he, William, should have the name of king, and that all things in the kingdom should be ruled by Ansgar.

More than anything else these transactions tell of the position London occupied in the eyes of the Normans. It was not her military but her constitutional position which was the essential thing. Her sheriff, the two orders of her citizens, the primates and optimates and the commonalty, stand out as definite parties to the understanding. William recognized that London was an institution in the country if not of the country, which it was necessary for him to master, and he could only become master by first of all being an ally. The destruction of London. if he could have accomplished it, would have done little for him. Its adhesion to his cause meant everything for him. It made him king of the land.

To understand this we must go back once more. It could not have been accomplished by a civic organization which had been built up by Anglo-Saxons out of the ruins of an older organization. It was not, as we know, their peculiar gift so to construct city life. There must have been a strong unified city government based upon forms which had come down from the only possible source of such forms, namely Roman London, and upon traditions and practice which would insure the stability of the forms The London with which William the Conqueror negotiated was a great institution as well as a great military stronghold—a greater institution than a military stronghold. and it is the neglect of this important fact which has led to much misconception of the place occupied by London at the beginning of Norman rule.

London, then, was to the Normans a great power in the land, a great institution. They proceeded to turn the power to their advantage, and to make the institution of national instead of local significance. The freedom of London from a dominating sovereign-power during the centuries of Anglo-Saxon rule was going to be the force which would make London fight for freedom whenever a sovereign-king strove for tyrannical power It was going to be the force which, coupled with the necessary sovereignty of the state, would create a municipal institution of far more importance to civilization than anything which had preceded it. It was going to be the force which would lead democratic communities to learn self-government. And if the Normans did not grasp all that was meant by these great forces in their incipient stage, they grasped quite easily the fact that London was to them the key-note to the development of England into a European state.

CHAPTER XII

THE GRIP OF THE NORMANS

WHATEVER Ansgar the sheriff and the governing authority of London thought they were gaining for London's independence on the old lines by the treaty with William, they soon found themselves in an entirely new position. After the crowning at Westminster in old Anglo-Saxon fashion, William did two things of great significance—one military, the other constitutional, and both having the same object, and as it turned out, the same result, namely, the subjection of London to the state. These two things were the building of a fortress on the very borders of the city but outside its civic jurisdiction, and the issue of a charter granting rights to the citizens. By these two actions the grip of the Normans was effectively closed upon London.

The first information we get about the great fortress is that William sent forward a portion of his conquering army with orders to prepare a fortress in or near London. The site, no doubt, of this earliest attempt was practically that of the present Tower of London The earliest attempt gave way to a more definite scheme later on. Displacing a section of the Roman wall including two towers next to the Thames, William commenced his work by constructing at first a deep ditch and strong palisade. About twelve or fourteen

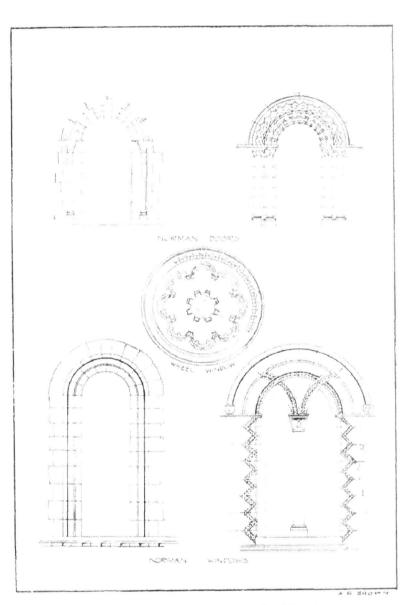

NORMAN DOORS

WHEEL WINDOW

NORMAN WINDOWS

A.B. BROWN

years later, that is about 1080, there was begun the magnificent keep which has remained ever since the central part of the whole group and has caused the whole to pass under the name of the Tower Later sovereigns, William Rufus, Henry II, Henry III, and Edward III, added the walls and the other towers. But from the first Londoners were taught to understand that this great fortress, situated between their city and the river-way to the open sea, was not so much a defence of London as an overawing power against London.

These facts make it quite clear that the grip of the Normans upon London was first expressed by their building of the Tower. London was never. as other castle towns were, a unity of castle and town, the castle's lord and the lord's citizens From the very first there was a division between the two. The city of London was the citizen's city, the Tower was the king's, outside the city area. The city of London was governed by its own institutions; the Tower represented the sovereign-government of the state And these two institutions were always in contrast, always at feud, always claiming and defending rights and privileges, the city against the Tower. From these significant facts we obtain one branch of the evidence of the original independence of London and of the grip the Normans fastened on it.

We get the second branch of evidence in another direction, namely, the grant of a charter. There was no charter in Anglo-Saxon times. There was no need for it. William's charter comes into history suddenly, called for by no demand from the citizens, expressing no changes in citizen-life or government, but doing

TOWER OF LONDON. THE WHITE TOWER.

one great and significant thing, namely, setting forth the will of the king.

The charter is as follows :—

William, King, greets William. bishop and Gosfrith portreeve, and all the burghers within London, French and English. friendly ; and I do you to wit that I will that ye be all law worthy that were in King Edwards day. And I will that every child be his fatheis heir after his fathers day. And I will not endure that any man offer any wrong to you. God keep you.

A noble document this has always been considered. And it is noble. But its significance has been wholly misunderstood. It is a grant of what the city already possessed, its laws and customs, and in particular its laws of inheritance to property which we have already seen differed so fundamentally from the English laws on the subject and which were inherited from Roman law. What, then, is the value of this new fangled instrument promulgated by the king? The value is to the king, not to the city. Hitherto the city had governed itself untouched by a king's hand except when it wanted its law to have legal force in parts beyond its own jurisdiction, as in the case of the Athelstan law. Now it had to be governed by the will of the sovereign. The essential significance of the chaitei is not what it grants, but the fact of the grant itself. 'I will' is the governing force of this charter, and when we come to trace out the details of all successive charters, it becomes abundantly clear that their object was to bring under the power of sovereign law what was previously held by municipal law.

Military force and sovereign power are, therefore, the two elements constituting the grip of the Normans

WESTMINSTER ABBEY.

upon London. It was a hard grip. Londoners did not probably understand it altogether at first. Understanding was brought home to them in succeeding generations, as we shall presently see. The Tower at their very doors was visible and understandable. The charter at their vitals was intangible and only a formality. But the charter changed the position of the city in the national constitution.

CHAPTER XIII

NORMAN LONDON

THE London which the Normans created was an altogether different London from that which they entered in 1066. They came to it friendliwise; they remained in it as conquerors. But they were magnificent conquerors. They found in the great city buildings of Roman origin doing duty for English purposes, and they found many decayed and destroyed parts The city had been sadly buffeted and torn during the centuries which witnessed the Anglo-Saxon encompassing and occupation, the Danish assault and conquest, and the varied events recorded and unrecorded which brought it finally under Norman rule.

When London was under Norman rule, however, it sprang into a place of beauty and renown. The Normans tolerated no ugliness or squalor if they could help it. They would use the ruins of the Roman wall and the foundations of Roman temples and buildings to erect a fortress wall of their own type, and churches and castellated buildings for their own purposes. And this they did right quickly and magnificently, for we have the well-known account of Fitzstephen, written in the twelfth century, only a hundred years after their entry into the city, and we have some of the remains of their buildings.

We will take Fitzstephen's account first. It is a

well-known document, but cannot be too well known, and I shall quote some of his narrative as translated by Sir Walter Besant.

It hath on the east part a tower Palatine, very large and very strong, whose court and walls rise up from a deep foundation. On the west are two castles well fenced. The wall of the city is high and great, continued with seven gates which are made double, and on the north distinguished with turrets by spaces. Likewise on the south London hath been enclosed with walls and towers, but the great river of Thames, well stored with fish, and in which the tide ebbs and flows by continuance of time, hath washed, worn away, and cast down those walls. Farther above in the west part the King's Palace is eminently seated upon the river, an incomparable building having a wall before it and some bulwarks. It is two miles from the city, continued with a suburb full of people.'

Here is the typical walled city of mediaeval times, the walled city which contained a community having a civic mind and action, and which used its walls for defence against the marauder who was sometimes the king, sometimes a faction of the nobility, sometimes the dissatisfied mob, and sometimes the rebel. All these enemies of peaceful citizenship were actively engaged during Norman and Plantagenet times. They made citizen life something more than mere industrialism or commercialism. They made it a burghal life, whereby military defence of the city constituted a full part of the daily routine of city work, and military defence meant mutual action and thought, the sacrifice of the good of the individual for the communal good.

NAVE OF ST. BARTHOLOMEW THE GREAT, WEST SMITHFIELD.

But London was specially constituted by its Norman owners, and there is nowhere else in Britain, and, I believe, nowhere else on the Continent, the special characteristics which belong to London. The Tower described by Fitzstephen was wholly the king's. It is worth while emphasizing this point here. The Tower is not in the city of London geographically, and it is entirely outside its jurisdiction. From the first the Tower of London was the king's. The city of London, pre-eminently the citizens' city, was within citizens' walls, was adjoining to, but not otherwise connected with, the Tower and when we come to Plantagenet times we shall see these significant building facts leading up to equally significant constitutional facts. This clear demarcation between castle and town is very important. If it indicates the king's will to command the city, it indicates, too, the citizens' resolve that he shall not do so from within the city. If it is Norman fashion to blend castle and town together, it is London fashion to keep them apart. And so they have ever been apart. The Tower of London is state property and is entirely under state control. The city of London is citizens' property and is entirely under municipal control, with privileges, customs, rights, and duties, such as no other city in the kingdom possesses.

But all of Norman London is a unity in one great respect—its architecture. There are not many remains of it left now. Fire and the centuries have had their influence upon even the solid magnificence of the Normans. But we can still stand in the beautiful chapel of the Tower, and in the round church of the Temple ; we can still go from these to the choir of St. Bartholomew, Smithfield and still walk under the

TOWER OF LONDON, ST. JOHN'S CHAPEL, IN THE KEEP.

beautiful arch in the cloisters of Westminster Abbey.
We may, too, still discover fragments of Norman work
in church crypts as at Westminster, in church columns
as in St. Saviour's, we may still pause before a single
arch or other building fragment which proclaims the
beauty of the structure of which it is but the last relic.
And we may place in our museums fragments of discovered capitals and other parts of Norman masonry
from the ruined architecture of the period. But we
cannot restore Norman London, either in descriptive
narrative or in descriptive art. That is gone from us,
and we have to leave Tewkesbury, Durham, Sherborne,
Romsey, and other places to tell us by analogy something of what London must have been in Norman
times.

Yet we know it was a beautiful, a very beautiful city.
Fitzstephen tells us that 'concerning the worship of
God in the Christian faith there are in London and in
the suburbs thirteen greater conventual churches,
besides 126 lesser parish churches'. There were 'three
famous schools at three principal churches, St. Paul's,
the Holy Trinity, and St Martin's'; and then he goes
on to describe the system of teaching adopted at
these schools, the quips and cranks, the discussions
and disputations by which 'the hearers, prepared for
laughter, make themselves merry in the meantime'.

Then we are told that 'almost all Bishops, Abbots,
and Noblemen of England are, as it were, citizens and
freemen of London. There they have fair dwellings,
and thither they do often resort and lay out a great
deal of money, and are called into the city to consulta-
tions and solemn meetings either by the King or their
metropolitan, or drawn by their own business'

One other extract will complete the constructive picture of the city. 'To this city merchants bring us wares by ships from every nation under heaven. The Arabian sends his gold, the Sabean his frankincense and spices, the Scythian arms, oil of palms from the plentiful wood, Babylon her fat soil, and Nilus his precious stones, the Seres send purple garments, they of Norway and Russia trouts, furs, and sables, and the French their wines.'

This description of London commerce in the twelfth century is the description of London at the present time. The figures and the places would be different, but the description might remain. It was not, however, all of Norman creation. The predecessors of the Norman had been at work on this great city. The Norman had embellished it and brought it to the requirements of its time. Norman London was Roman London with additions necessary for its future development.

CHAPTER XIV

THE FIRST GREAT LONDONERS

THERE have always been traditions of great Londoners. King Lud, Belinus, and a number of other names occur in the earliest period without, however, much chance of ever becoming anything further than mere names. Nevertheless it is not improbable that in the place-names of London there lurks the last fragment of a biography which if we possessed it in full, would be of untold interest and value. Inscriptions and potters' marks of Roman times contain more likely memorials of resident Londoners, though of course they principally tell us of the manufacturers who sent their products to London. Of the Roman names associated with London it is impossible to pick out even one who might be called a Londoner in any strict sense of the term, and Kemble has put this fact into strongly-worded sentences which on the whole seem to be quite true. · We seek in vain for any evidence of the Romanized Britons having been employed in any offices of trust or dignity or permitted to share in the really valuable results of civilization, there is no one Briton recorded of whom we can confidently assert that he held any position of dignity and power under the Roman rule; the historians, the geographers, nay even the novelists, are here consulted in vain, nor in the many inscriptions which we possess relating to Britain can we point

out a single British name.'[1] Certainly therefore we
cannot point to a London name. The Welsh traditions
point somewhat strongly to London men having played
a great part in national affairs after the Romans had
ceased to govern their province of Britain, but even so
the actual names escape us, and the roll of Anglo-Saxon
bishops only enables us to identify one Londoner,
Nothelm, archbishop of Canterbury and the friend of
Bede, who is said to have been London born   Throughout the Anglo-Saxon Chronicle the Londoners, the
citizens of London, the chief men of London, play an
important part; but they are nearly all nameless.
Deorman of London held lands at Islington according
to Domesday. William, in a charter, calls him 'Deorman
my man', and Mr. Round draws attention to the fact
that 'Theim son of Deorman' was a witness to a
charter by Geoffrey de Mandeville—evidence of riches
and influence perhaps, but of nothing further. Two
place-names may contain personal names—'Coel-
mundinge haga' and 'Hwaetmundes stone'[2] but we
are still only in the presence of names, not persons.
The *Onomasticon Anglo-Saxonicum* sets before us a
bewildering list of names, most of which are nothing
more than *nomina virorum*, and it is only when we come
to the moneyers that the hope of identifying a Londoner
is strong. Thus the fine list of Edward the Confessor's
moneyers contains names which are found on London
coins only, and such special names as 'Ælffet', 'Glif-
wine', 'Goldan', 'Wirema', and some others, perhaps
bring us into touch with real Londoners.

Before we can arrive at anything like a living

[1] *Saxons in England*, ii 280.
[2] T

personality of London, however, we have to travel far
down the centuries, and the first great Londoner to
emerge is Ansgar, sheriff in the fateful year 1066.
There is very little known of Ansgar, but all that is
known is so great—great Londoner, great Englishman, great statesman, great patriot, and one's mind
goes out to him, one is almost glad that he is the first
Londoner whom we can identify by name.   He is
Londoner by right of office, for he was Sheriff of London
and Middlesex, and he led forth the men of London to
the great fight at Hastings, led them to their proud place
as guard to the king himself and his standard.   How
he fought there we know, not by the reports of
personal prowess but by the records of the whole
battle fought from morning until sundown, and from
the fact that he returned to the city sore wounded,
'disabled by honourable wounds,' as Mr Freeman
translates the contemporary record.[1]   He could neither
walk nor ride, but was carried about the city in a
litter   Then comes another and important event, the
action of London after the defeat at Hastings   It
declared for resistance ; a gemot was held within its
walls, and it elected Eadgar to be king   And when
the Londoners found that Eadgar was not worthy,
they consented to negotiate with William.   Throughout all these transactions—constitutional resistance
to the invader, independence of action, we can trace
the hands of strong men; and Ansgar, there is no doubt,
was the leader of these strong men, for William at
last agreed to terms which made Ansgar of London
the chief man in the kingdom under King William.
Indeed, Ansgar is spoken of as being the soul of all

the counsels taken by the defenders of London There
is not a single episode of these most fateful events
which does not bear witness, albeit silent witness, to
the greatness of Ansgar. He fought for the Anglo-
Saxon king. He supported an Anglo-Saxon successor.
He stood up to the mightiest soldier and statesman
of the time to claim for London her pride of place
in the kingdom as soon as he knew that the kingdom
was destined to pass into the hands of this great man.
No faltering and no paltering. All strength, that is
Ansgar's record—a record that belongs to the first
known Londoner

Great names do not crowd upon us even after this.
Normans had succumbed to the fascination of London,
and were more of Londoners than the Londoners
themselves.   There is ample evidence of this—
evidence how they intermarried with Londoners,
evidence how they made London their chosen home,
how they entered into the government of London.
how they lived its life, fought for its rights, defended
its privileges, created new rights and privileges incidental to their freshly created positions, and generally
conducted themselves as great pioneers of a new
movement always conduct themselves when determined to carve out for themselves new lives in new
homes.   It is difficult to give a collective account of
these men or to dwell upon the events with which
they were associated.   We have not all the names.
Accident preserves some of them in obscure documents which demand the investigation of specialist
scholars before the significance of such records can be
properly gauged, but the chroniclers of the day are
not favourable to names.   They relate the doings of

their own party and perhaps the heroes of the events affecting their own party. They leave in significant silence much that happened and the names of those who took part in opposition to themselves. We thus get an incomplete story so far as personages are concerned, and we cannot adequately relate even parts of that story.

Ansgar was succeeded in his office of staller by Geoffrey de Mandeville the first of that name, whose grandson as lord of the Tower of London played so conspicuous and so sorry a figure under Stephen and under Maud, and who betrayed his hatred, as Mr. Round puts it, for those upstarts. as they were deemed, the royal justices , and who, on Mr Round's evidence, over-awed the Londoners by his command of the Tower when he was, against the wishes of the Londoners, assisting the Empress Maud. Another prominent personage standing out as a Londoner in a more special sense was Gervase of Cornhill, who carried on a mercantile and money-lending business, which was fortunately the subject of some scornful remarks against the trader and all his works by a contem-porary writer of Stephen's reign. These men are worth mentioning because of the prominent part played by London in the settlement of that 'election' to the crown which has made the reign of Stephen so valuable to constitutional historians

Gervase of Cornhill was great in two ways, personally because of the man, locally because of the association with a London name still in being Mr. Round has brought his great skill in historical research to bear upon Gervase, and he identifies him with *Gervasius filius Rogeri nepotis Huberti* who figures prominently

on the Pipe Roll of 1130 (31 Hen. I); with Gervase.
Justiciary of London, who meets us twice under
Stephen, with Gervase, who was one of the sheriffs
of London in 1155 and 1156. This prominent Londoner married Agnes, daughter of Godeleve and
Edward de Cornhill, thus giving us one great example
of Norman settlers in London intermarrying with the
English stock. Gervase appears, from the charters
which Mr. Round has examined so carefully, to have
lent money on mortgage and to have acquired landed
property by foreclosing, and Mr. Round thinks that he
may have been that Gervase who at the head of the
citizens of London met Henry II in 1174. He lived
on till 1183, and was probably at his death seventy or
seventy-five years old.[1]

Passing by mere names we come to a greater and
a more real Londoner from a charter by Geoffrey of
Mandeville, granted, Mr. Round thinks, as an act of
restitution while he was lying on his death-bed in
1144. This is Gilbert Becket, 'Gileberto Beket,' the
earliest mention of this name on record, which takes
us to the magnate of London hailing from Rouen and
living in Cheapside, where his great son, Thomas à
Becket, 'archbishop, saint and martyr,' was born.
Henry II's struggle with the great London-born priest
is chiefly known from priest-written chronicles, but
even so there appears the beginning of that long con-
tention between the English State and the Roman
Church which only ended with the Reformation The
great archbishop fought for his church, the great king
for his kingdom; and no one who reads Bishop
Stubbs's masterly and discriminating summary of these

[1] Rou (⸱ ⸱ 10

transactions can doubt that the Church, as represented by Archbishop Thomas à Becket of London, was in the wrong. We can say this now from the distance that time gives to historical judgements, and because we look back to it from the years of later ages instead of forward to it from the years of earlier times; but we can also render tribute to this great Londoner of Norman domination.

CHAPTER XV

THE GRIP OF THE PLANTAGENETS

THE grip of the Normans was a conqueror's grip. The grip of the Plantagenets was that of the statesman—far more deadly to ancient conditions, far more sure of intending changes. London under the Conqueror was occupied in absorbing the Normans, while the Normans were becoming fascinated by the great city. The Plantagenets brought the city inside the nation, teaching the nation to recognize the city and the city to become welded with the nation. The Plantagenet work was a great work, albeit done roughly and perhaps brutally at moments when monarchs and statesmen set about what they had to do in a fashion to serve their own ends, not seeing that their own ends were the vital political ends of the period—that the individual mind had become attuned to the common thought. We cannot in a small compass gather together all the evidence of this, but there are sufficient illustrative examples.

There is, first of all, the evidence of the charters. What are charters granted by the sovereign monarch to cities? They do not create the city; they do not in the earlier cases settle the constitution of the city. These negations of purpose are extremely important because they raise the question as to what their positi   .   .   '   .   '   A. 1 it pears

to me that all the great historical authorities who have
examined and expounded these precious documents
have misunderstood their significance. Charters to
London are in a somewhat different category from
charters to other cities. They gradate from the
general recognition of rights in William's charter to
the detailed recognition of further rights in successive
charters, and I have endeavoured in my book on *The
Governance of London* to point out how this gradation
occurs and what it exactly means.   What I think was
happening was that the crown authority was discovering the value of these rights, and only gradually
discovering their value, and it would not do to allow
rights of value to rest on any other basis than that of
the sovereign will.   There thus arose the practice
of charters being granted to the cities, and when these
are examined carefully it is found that over and over
again they are not granting new rights, rights that
did not previously exist, but under the guise of a grant
of rights they were bringing within the fold of charter
legislation rights which were already being exercised
as municipal law   In this way municipal law, which
was so much in advance of state law, was gradually
being caught up by state law.   The state was gradually
building up its control and powers over the cities by
a species of legislation by charters.   And that this was
accomplished gradually is shown in a remarkable
manner by one special case   This is the slow compre-
hension by the state of the fact that within the state were
various communities of persons who held lands in their
collective capacity, and that this holding of lands was
not in accord with the individualistic policy of the state.
How could a group of people hold lands?   To whom

did the lands belong—who would perform the military
and feudal duties, who would be responsible therefor
to the state? These questions were settled by specific
legislation In 1279 a statute was passed by which no
religious bodies were to acquire land, but it took more
than a century beyond this for the state to discover
that there were civil as well as religious communities
who held lands, and so in 1391 there was passed
a disabling act by which municipal bodies were made
to understand that they could not acquire property
unless they were incorporated by the crown as a legal
person, and thus acquired the right. All this is highly
technical perhaps, but the story of the charters is an
essential feature of the grip which the Plantagenets
obtained upon London. London under the Plantagenets passed out of the position of a more or less
independently organized city to a city which had
become part and parcel of the new state of England.

There is next the evidence of the sokes, those independent jurisdictions which appear in Norman times.
but which had definite life in Plantagenet times.
Henry I had granted in his charter that 'the churches
and barons and citizens may have and hold quietly
and in peace their sokes with all their customs', and
I translate this to mean that the Normans carved
out for themselves little islands of jurisdiction which
they governed unrestricted by any external control
except that of the king. Under Norman rule these
sokes were encroachments upon municipal unity. But
they helped to make the Norman sokemen Londoners.
and when the Plantagenet had his grip upon London
these sokemen had become Londoners. The sokes tried
to assume the position of manors within the city, but

with it all there was the 'communio quam vocant Londoniarum', which, with the jurisdictional unity in folkmoot and husting, as Miss Bateson has so well said, proclaimed the municipal unity of London.

An important economical feature of Plantagenet London is the aggregation of industrial centres in the city. Fitzstephen says that 'men of all trades, sellers of all sorts of wares, labourers in every work, every morning are in their distinct and several places', and we get the following results ·

Eastcheap = mercers and haberdashers.

Old Exchange = goldsmiths.

Sopers Lane = peppers and grocers.

Lombard Street = drapers.

St. Mary Axe = skinners

Thames Street = fishmongers.

Ironmongers Lane = ironmongers.

Vinetree = vintners.

Stockesmarket = butchers.

Hosiers Lane = hosiers

Cordwayner Street = shoemakers and curriers.

Poultry = poulterers

Paternoster Row = stationers.

Cornhill = corn market.

This is the place to deal with the constitutional position of the Tower of London, whose special geographical position in relation to the city of London has already been described. In the thirteenth century considerable additions were made and a remarkable story is told by Matthew Paris, the chronicler, of the year 1241, which illustrates in a forceful manner the feelings of Londoners—not the feelings of the moment, but the settled convictions of generations—towards the Tower

St. Thomas the Martyr. 'a Londoner by birth,' is said
to have appeared to a priest, carrying a cross in his
hands, and regarding the walls, which the king had at
that time built, with a scowling look, made it known that
he considered these walls 'were built as an insult and
to the prejudice of the Londoners'. The citizens are
said to have regarded these walls 'as a thorn in their
eyes, and they had heard the taunts of the people, who
said that these walls had been built as an insult to
them, and that if any one of them should dare to con-
tend for the liberty of the city he would be shut up in
them and consigned to imprisonment'. These building traditions would be valuable if they stood alone.
They stand, as a matter of fact, in front of the constitutional aspect, to which reference may now be made.

We have it on record that the citizens made definite
rules to govern their conduct in the case of the Tower
It was the seat of the king's justice. Upon the day
on which the pleas of the crown were held. the citizens
met at Barking Church and proceeded to the Tower in
solemn array, 'six or more of the more serious honourable and discreet barons of the city are to enter the
Tower for the purpose of saluting and welcoming his
lordship the king his council and justiciars on behalf
of the city; begging of them that if it so please his
lordship the king, they may safely appear before them
in the said Tower saving all their liberties and customs
unto the Mayor and all other citizens.'[1] Another rule
is still more illustrative of the attitude of the citizen
towards the Tower. 'Injunctions should be given to
the two Aldermen whose wards are nearest to the
Tower to the effect that upon the third day before the

[1] Compare *Liber Albus* (Riley Trans.) 17–53

pleas of the crown are holden they must enter the
Tower for the purpose of examining the benches in
the great hall to see if they are sound ; and if they
should happen to be broken they must cause the same
to be well and strongly repaired.'   And then there is
the injunction to ' have a strong bench made in the
middle of the hall opposite the great seat of his lordship the king ', upon which the mayor and barons of
the city were to be seated, when making answer to the
king as to matters pertaining to the crown   The
citizens were also to have their own porter without the
gate of the Tower, their own usher without the door of
the Hall. their own serjeants with their wands—not
all ceremonial in these days, but significant of rights
and privileges   Such rights and privileges were being
fought for all along the line   'The Mayor of London ',
it is recorded in the *Liber Albus*, ' did not act under
the king's commission at the delivery of the Gaol of
Newgate or at the determining of any pleas touching
the crown in reference to any cases whatsoever that
might arise within the said city unless perchance it
had become a custom with the mayors to sue for such
royal commissions without prejudice and not as an
acknowledgement of any superior right'   Here is the
assertion of a definite claim, and the city's rights were
being regained under the Plantagenets from the Normans who had overawed them, regained in constitutional fashion as constitutional acts by a city constitutionally representing a portion of the state.   There is
curious evidence of this in a legal case of 38 Edward III
wherein Wm Ffinishingfeild was found guilty of an
assault upon Nicholas Turgeis ' without the forraine
gate of the Towie and within the liberties of the same '

in the court of 'Hoistinge', London, 'as though the
place where the transgression' was made 'had been
within the lybertyes of the Citty'. At this pre-
sumption 'the King took displeasure' and granted
a commission to 'reforme the Recordes'.[1]

It may be well to compare these details of city
governance and care of rights with another example.
In 1465 'was the sergeaunts fest and the maire of
London should have dyned there; and bicause the
chief place was not kepte for him while the kyng was
not there nor of his blode, he came away with alle his
compeigny of this cite and dyned at home in his owne
place'.

Of the citizens' walls—the property of the citizens—
there is special care, and a specimen record of how they
were kept in repair is worth quoting. 'This yere the
Mayr and the Comons began to Repayre the walles of
the city and to clense the Diches of the same : and for
to bere the charge there he caused to be graunted by
Comon Counseill, that euery citezein shud pay euery
sonday duryng his yere vd. And aboue that, he by
his politik meanys caused dyvers ffelyshippes of worship to make euery ffelishp a certayn length of the
walle ; and to Encorage theym he began wt his owne
ffelyship which made the wall from Allhalou in the
wall vnto Bisshoppysgate ; and like wyse other ffeli-
shippys theyr partes ; and or his yere came to ende he
had made a goode parte of that which is newe made
beside provysion of lyme and Bryk, which he also pro-
vyded for in the more the same yere.' This patriotic
mayor was Rauf Joslyn, and we have the spirit of the

[1] *Hist MSS Commission*, vii. 591. What the process of 'reforming
the records' was I do not know.

times revealing itself in the words of the chronicle narrative   But there is closer record than this for in 1458 ' was a grete watch in London and al the gates kept every nyght and ij aldermen watchyng ', a picture of burghal life which is full of meaning to those who will trouble to understand its significance.   Citizen walls mean citizen military organization, and London possessed this down to late days.   Matthew Paris lets us into a knowledge of the system in his record that the third division of the army of the barons in 1264 was composed of Londoners commanded by Nicholas Segrave, but a remarkable document temp. Henry VIII, setting forth the muster of the citizens for the midsummer watch ' as in tyme past hath bene accustomed ', gives the full detail.   ' When ev'y thyng was redy, ev'y alderman by hymself musteryd hys owne warde yn the fields, vewyng theym in harnes and sawe that ev'y man had a sworde and a dagger and suche as were not meate to be archars were turnyd to pykes and theyre bowes delyv'ed to such as were mete to be archars.'   The description goes on to say that on the 8th of May every alderman with his ward in good order of battle before six o'clock in the morning came into the common field between ' Myle End and Whyte Chapell ', that field which, as we have noted already, originated with the Roman organization of the city, and kept on according to ancient and continued custom until these late times [1]

Some details of the mob brutality and of the Court brutality will not give too lurid a light upon Plantagenet London, and I will quote Bishop Stubbs.   On October 15, 1326 the city broke out into rebellion

[1] *Archaeologia*, xxxii. 33

over the Despencer troubles. One unfortunate man, John le Marchal, a citizen who was regarded as a spy of the Despencers, was caught in his inn in Walbrook, dragged into Cheap, stripped and beheaded. Just at this time the unfortunate Bishop Stapleton, who had been visiting his new house outside Temple Bar, came riding into the city with two of his squires, William Wall, who was his nephew, and John of Paddington, the latter being steward of the new mansion. He entered the city by Newgate, and on his way to the Tower was to stay in Old Dean's Lane to take his noonday meal He had reached the church of St. Michael le Quern, which stood at the west end of Cheapside near the cross. Hearing the cries of 'Traitor! traitor!' he turned his horse and attempted to reach St. Paul's, but at the north door he was seized, dismounted, and dragged into the Cheap through the middle of St. Paul's Churchyard and there stripped and beheaded, with a panade or butcher's knife which one of the bystanders offered, by a certain R. de Hatfield. The bishop's two squires perished with him.

There are indeed some gruesome notes of the City's struggle with the Court. Thus in 1440 it is recorded that ' the last day of August in fletestrete ther was a grete debate by the nyght tyme bitwene men of Courte and men of London. Where thurgh shotte of bowes, as in londe of Werre, of both parties there were many men hurt fowle and slayne; and one called William herbotell a man of Courte, Beyng principall cause of all that mysgouernaunce '—a misgovernaunce which according to the Chronicle was repeated next year—'and M. Roger was drawyn vnto

Tiborn and ther was hanged, hedid, and quartred
Howbeit he there toke it vpon his deth he died giltles
of that he died for'. In 1458 also 'was a greate affray
in fletestrete bitwene men of Courte and Inhabytauntes
of the same strete. In which affiay the Quenys
attourney was slayn'.

Thus it will be gathered that the grip of the
Plantagenet was not a tender grip. Strong and constitutional it was in a special manner, rude and
barbarous it also was in a general way. Men were
killed with little regard to the sentiment of human
life executed for crimes they were hastily assumed to
have committed, killed in the streets without warning,
butchered without mercy or consideration. And yet,
reading through the evidence as a whole one must
recognize that Plantagenet times were good times for
London—were necessary times for its evolution from
a city with claims to independence to a city with
claims to recognition as a constitutional unit of a well-
founded and well-organized state.

CHAPTER XVI

PLANTAGENET LONDON

IT is difficult to recall Plantagenet London Churches, monasteries, and other ecclesiastical foundations occupied about one quarter of its area. All the great nobles had residences there. The king possessed a residence within its walls. Merchants were rich and powerful and their homes were elaborate and extensive. The streets were narrow and the walls were kept in good repair It must have been a crowded place but not altogether a wholesome place, for in the *Chronicle of London*, edited by Sir Harris Nicolas, it is recorded of the year 1415 that ' was mad newe g'tes at London Wall and a new gate, and the prevy that stod withinne the more was drawe doun and set on this syde of the wall over the comoum dych that comyth out of the more'.

But after all, the principal examples of Plantagenet structure which remain to us refer to a London developing outside the city walls. These are of course the magnificent Westminster Hall, one of the most beautiful specimens of mediaeval architecture, with the beautiful 1292 crypt of St. Stephen's Chapel still intact, and the Abbey Church of Westminster, one of the glories of our country. It is impossible to consider their position outside London and all that this means without recognizing it as a feature of the

ST. PAUL'S CATHEDRAL AT THE PRESENT DAY.

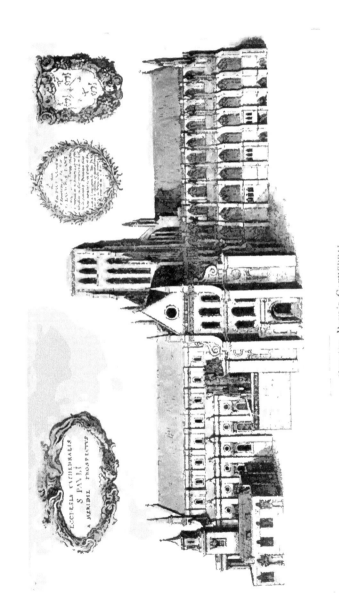

Old St. Paul's Cathedral.

EAST WINDOW OF ST. ETHELREDA'S CHAPEL, ELY PLACE, HOLBORN.

mediaeval city which (always a remarkable characteristic of Anglo-Saxon London) was again tending to
develop under the Plantagenets. The city was not independent of its surroundings, as it was in the earlier
period ; but under a new form of municipal development its surroundings became an essential part of
its life.

Of other buildings of the Plantagenet period outside the city the most interesting is perhaps Lambeth
Palace, the residence of the Archbishops of Canterbury. The chapel is the oldest part, dating from the
thirteenth century. The so-called Lollards' Tower at
the west end of the chapel is of the early fifteenth
century, and the rest of the building is the product
of many hands at varying dates. The hall of Lincoln's
Inn is another example of remains of Plantagenet
London beyond the city. And then we have the
beautiful hall of Eltham Palace, dating from the
fourteenth century, and of course much further afield,
to tell us of the surrounding beauties of London.

The Savoy Chapel, last relic of a prince's palace on
the river-side in the Strand (remains of thirteenth
century), the Chapel of St. Ethelreda, last relic of
a bishop's palace at Ely Place, Holborn (fourteenth
century), and the houses fronting the north side of
Staple Inn (fifteenth century), an Inn of Chancery, so
called because of its proximity to the staples which
formed Holborn Bars, the limit of the city lands outside
the gate, are the remaining examples of domestic architecture left to us from this period. The Church of
St. Thomas Apostle, Southwark, was the church of the
dissolved monastery of St. Thomas in Southwark, dating
from the fourteenth century. St. John's Gate, Clerken-

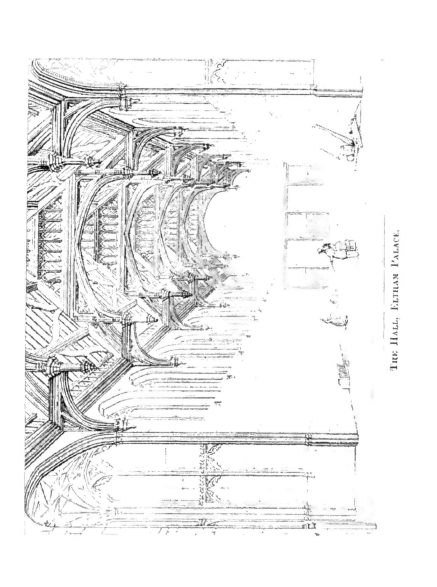

THE HALL, ELTHAM PALACE.

St. Luke's Church, Chelsea.

well, is the southern gateway of the Priory, and was built in 1504, but the beautiful crypt is of the twelfth century St. Luke's Church, Chelsea, dates in its oldest portions from the fourteenth century. St Margaret's. Westminster, is of the fifteenth century : St. Dunstan, Stepney, dates from the fourteenth century. These are the only early churches, and it is singular that so few examples of early churches remain in the counties round London. It is the least-equipped area in this respect of any in England, and we have to take into account the craze for rebuilding and destruction which was indulged in by architects at the expense of the beautiful The story is a deplorable one Over and over again do we read not only of destruction but of senseless destruction. A church is rebuilt. a hall is pulled down, as it would appear, for the mere sake of architectural experiment, never satisfactory when it has been accomplished. And in our own recent days we have had to deplore the destruction of Crosby Hall, not only a beautiful place of itself but a place which might have been considered sacred to the memory of Shakespeare, for Shakespeare undoubtedly stood within its walls and under its noble roof.

Turning to the city itself, some of the churches escaped the great fire, and there are also fragments of the city Halls discoverable behind the modern structures. Of these latter the beautiful Early English remains in Merchant Taylors' Hall and the remains in Mercers' Hall are the most noted. Clifford's Inn dates from the fourteenth century. The Church of St. Ethelburga in Bishopsgate Street : St. Giles', Cripplegate ; St. Helen's, Bishopsgate Street

Within (formerly the Church of the Priory of the
Nuns of St. Helen's); St. Catherine Cree (remains of
ancient masonry along the south and west fronts);
St. Olave, Hart Street, All Hallows, Barking, 'the most
complete mediaeval church in London'; the nave of
Austin Friars' Church in Old Broad Street, have all
come to us through the dangers of the Great Fire
from Plantagenet times.

The Guildhall, though destroyed in the Great Fire,
has preserved some of its early fifteenth-century work,
dating, no doubt, from the building recorded in the
Chronicle of London, edited by Sir Harris Nicolas, of
the year 1411, that 'this yere the Yeldhalle of London
was begonne to make newe'. Only quite recently
Mr. Sydney Perks, the city surveyor, has uncovered
some delightful architectural features of the early
building, and the crypt is a very fine piece of work
worthy of Plantagenet London. The Guildhall is the
symbol of Plantagenet municipal rule—that rule which
fought the sovereign, kept up municipal traditions,
bowed to the inevitable development of state government, and handed down to Tudor times a city which
had not bowed its head to royal caprice.

To know our Plantagenet London we have to fill up
the gaps not occupied by buildings of the period, by
restoring in imagination similar buildings to the sites
now represented by later creations. Old St. Paul's, as
beautiful as Westminster Abbey Church, to replace
the present cathedral, fifteenth-century and earlier
churches to replace the creations of Wren and his
followers, rows of houses on the plan of Staple Inn,
palaces of the nobility and the princes of the Church,
as Lambeth or Eltham Palace is to-day, and imagina-

CHRIST'S HOSPITAL.
(From an engraving by Toms)

DOOR OF AN OLD MANSION IN GRAVEL LANE, HOUNDSDITCH.
(From an etching by J. W. Archer in 1851.)

tion can go but a short way towards what the reality must have been. We must add the gardens. In Bishopsgate, in Austin Friars, in Broad Street, in many odd places in the city, there were glorious gardens when Gerard the Herbalist wrote his great book in Elizabeth's reign, gardens which must have been formed in earlier times for them to have been so good in later days. Indeed there is direct evidence of this, as the reference to the 'houses and gardynes . . . down aboughte Poules' in 1372 in Sir Harris Nicolas's *Chronicle of London* (p. 68) will show, and they must have added to the beauty of the buildings to which they were adjuncts.

CHAPTER XVII

THE GREAT LONDONERS OF PLANTAGENET TIMES

IT is impossible to contemplate the doings of Plantagenet London without comprehending the greatness of the men who engaged in these doings. They were great in commerce, great in national politics, great in municipal politics, making many mistakes, performing many harsh and brutal actions, rushing after their own ends—but withal great men in the net result of building up their city to take its place in the new nation. They showed this in many ways, and perhaps the most picturesque example is the appeal made by Calais in 1436, when she was invested by the Duke of Burgundy. On the 27th of June the mayor and aldermen of Calais, being anxious to get help from the Government at home, and finding that according to precedent they could only do so through the mediation of the city of London, addressed a letter to the mayor and aldermen of London imploring them as the head of 'the principal of all the cities of the realm of England to move the King to send the requisite aid'. The mayor was Henry Frowyk, who got up a contingent to the relief of the town.[1] This is the kind of thing the mayors of London did in those days. A certain royalty of movement and of motive made them, as the head of a great city, representative of the position the city held in the polity of the period, and this is quite in keeping with what we have already discovered in the laws, the customs and the actions of the city. They were mayors in no mean sense They represented all the traditions. all the historic sense of the city, and one feels that as each successive mayor took up his position he took it up just where his predecessor left it, carrying on in the old fashion unalterable rules, allowing his personality to a large extent to sink beneath the weight of accumulated knowledge of what London expected its mayors to do, and of what its mayors gladly did in the great interests which were entrusted to their keeping.

Coming down the stream of time, there is the first mayor of London, who must have been a great personality. An early manuscript record, the *Liber de Antiquis Legibus*, preserved at the Guildhall, states that in the first year of the reign of King Richard (1188) 'Henry FitzEylwin of Londenestane was made mayor of London, who was the first mayor of the city, and continued to be such mayor to the end of his life, that is to say, for nearly five and twenty years'. That is a record that speaks for itself, not only the first mayor, but mayor for twenty-five years!

In reading of the doings of the city magnates we are watching proceedings which intertwine between municipal custom and state government Nicholas Wottone, mayor in 1416, was served with a writ bidding him reopen the windows of the house of Richard Anable. The mayor promptly replied to the effect that by immemorial custom any freeman of the ⁣⁣⁣ ⁣⁣ ⁣ ⁣ of the mayor and aldermen was deprived of the franchise and prevented from following any craft in the city, that Richard Anable had refused to obey an order to appear at the Guildhall on the 29th of October, 3 Henry V (1415), and was on that account removed from the franchise and forbidden to follow his craft, that nevertheless he continued to exercise his craft openly in his shop, and that thereupon the windows of his shop were closed and they could not be reopened without prejudice to the liberties of the city. These were drastic measures, and Nicholas Wottone, mayor, had to appear before the king's judges at Westminster, where he successfully defended the city law.[1] But let us note two things: first, that the governing authority of the city was mayor and aldermen, not the commonalty in folkmoot assembled, secondly, the attempted interference of the state law and its signal failure. Nicholas Wottone, mayor, was not the man to give away the rights of the city when they crossed the power of the state, and he is only typical of the Plantagenet mayors. I will quote one further example from the year 1417, when Richard Merlawe mayor, and the aldermen, being served with a writ directing them to take measures for the strict observance of the ordinance prescribing the particular kind of work to be executed severally by cordwainers and cobblers, replied that by immemorial custom of the city the mayor and aldermen were in the habit of causing any ordinance affecting artificers in the city, which proved to be prejudicial to the common good, to cease to be observed.[2] The mayor and aldermen were therefore the governing

[1] *Letter Book of the City Corporation*, i 156

authority in these matters, not the king and his courts of judges—and we cannot have better testimony to the nature of the struggle which these men of Plantagenet London had to face, a struggle which meant the constant cutting off from city law and custom of powers, inherited from a former condition of constitutional independence, and which could not be tolerated under constitutional sovereignty.

Among the names which stand out most conspicuously from Plantagenet times is that of Sir Richard Whityngton. Legend and romance have been busy with his name. This means that he was a great personality, a name with which Londoners used to conjure, for legend and romance do not associate themselves with the unheroic and the ordinary. Legend and romance, however, do not cover up recorded history, and it is abundantly clear that Whityngton, the youngest son of a Shropshire family, came to London probably penniless, entered a London mercer's house for employment, married his master's daughter, was elected alderman in 1393, was mayor in 1397, again in 1406 and 1419, and was member of Parliament in 1416. All his doings are magnificent. His charities were great and good. His munificence as mayor was proverbial, and when after Agincourt he entertained the soldier king and his bride Catherine of France, he took a packet of bonds from his breast and throwing them on the fire said, 'Thus do I acquit your Highness of a debt of £60,000,' for they were the security for a loan to the king for the prosecution of his war with France. This was real romance. He always seemed to do his good deeds with picturesque surroundings and thus romance was busy with his name to the end of his career. There is a curious drawing of his death-bed scene, one of his attendant friends being his executor, John Carpenter, the great town clerk of the city, who founded the City of London School. Romance wove into his life the familiar story of the cat, an attachment, as Mr. Wheatley has shown, from mediaeval legend—just the sort of attachment which an unread people would apply to the hero they hardly understood.

A hero of a different kind was the mayor. Sir William Walworth, who slew Wat Tyler in Smithfield—not a very gallant act of itself, and an act which might have become a very dangerous one if the young king had not turned the incident to good account. The scene is quaintly described by an unknown contemporary, in Anglo-French, and I will quote a few passages from Professor Oman's translation [1]

Then the King caused a proclamation to be made that all the commons of the country who were still in London should come to Smithfield to meet him there; and so they did.

And when the King and his train had arrived there, they turned into the eastern meadow in front of St. Bartholomew's, which is a house of canons, and the Commons arrayed themselves on the west side in great battles. At this moment the Mayor of London, William Walworth, came up, and the King bade him go to the Commons and ask their chieftain to come to him. And when he was summoned by the Mayor, by the name of Wat Tighler of Maidstone he came to the King with great confidence, mounted on a little horse, that the Commons might see him. And he dismounted, holding in his hand a dagger which he had taken from another man, and when he had dismounted, he half bent his knee, and then took the King by the hand, and shook his arm forcibly and roughly, saying to him, 'Brother, be of good comfort and joyful, for you shall have in the fortnight that is to come, praises from the Commons even more than you have yet had, and we shall be companions'. . . Then the King asked him what were the points which he wished to have revised and he should have them freely, without contradiction, written out and sealed. Thereupon the said Walter rehearsed the points which were to be demanded. . .

During all this time that the King was speaking, no lord or counsellor dared or wished to give answer to the Commons in any place save the King himself. Presently Wat Tighler, in the presence of the King, sent for a flagon of water to rinse his mouth, because of the great heat that he was in, and when it was brought, he rinsed his mouth in a very rude and disgusting fashion before the King's face. And then he bade them bring him a jug of beer, and drank a great draught, and then, in the presence of the King, climbed on his horse again. At this time a certain valet from Kent, who was among the King's retinue, asked that the said Walter, the chief of the Commons, might be pointed out to him. And when he saw him, he said aloud that he knew him for the greatest robber and thief in all Kent. Wat heard these words, and bade him come out to him, wagging his head at him in sign of malice; but the valet refused to approach, for fear that he had of the mob. But at last the lords made him go out to him to see what he (Wat) would do before the King. And when Wat saw him he ordered one of his followers, who was riding behind him carrying his banner displayed, to dismount and behead the said valet. But the valet answered that he had done nothing worthy of death, for what he had said was true, and he would not deny it, but he could not lawfully make debate in the presence of his liege-lord without l   e   p   d G   b   at he could do without reproof, for if he was struck he would strike back again. And for these words Wat tried to strike him with his dagger, and would have slain him in the King's presence; but because he strove to do so, the Mayor of London, William Walworth, reasoned with the said Wat for his violent behaviour and despite, done in the King's presence, and arrested him. And because he arrested him, the said Wat stabbed the Mayor with his dagger in the stomach in great wrath. But as it pleased God, the Mayor was wearing armour and took no harm, but like a hardy and vigorous man drew his cutlass, and struck back at the said Wat and gave him a deep cut on the neck, and then a great cut on the head. And during this scuffle one of the King's household drew his sword and ran Wat two or three times through the body, mortally wounding him And he spurred his horse, crying to the Commons to avenge him, and the horse carried him some fourscore paces, and then he fell to the ground half dead. And when the Commons saw him fall, and knew not how for certain it was, they began to bend their bows and shoot, wherefore the King himself spurred his horse and rode out to meet them, commanding them that they could all come to him at Clerkenwell Fields.

But we get huge lists of city magnates during the Plantagenet period, lists of mayors, lists of sheriffs, lists of aldermen and it is difficult to make selections when once we have noted the most generally famous There were men who stood up to the king for the city rights, there were men who stood up for the king for national rights; there were men who pursued their own ends—there were men of all sorts just as in modern times But these Plantagenet men on the whole stand out grandly. They were engaged in a great work and they did it in a great and magnificent way. They helped to weld the city and the state, but they did not in so doing sacrifice the city. They contributed largely to national funds for national purposes—grumbling of course at the exactions of the king, but contributing their money and frequently their sons. Ever active, these men of London deserve to be known to Londoners, for they were an example which Londoners of later ages might well emulate.

Above all things they stood for honesty in trade and commerce, and again we have to note that it was municipal, not state, law which governed these matters. The records of the early gilds are all good reading for many purposes. The plumbers enacted that ' every-one of the trade shall do his work well and lawfully ', and further that ' no one for any singular profit shall engross lead coming to the said city for sale to the damage of the commonalty, but that all persons of the same trade as well poor as rich who may wish shall be partners therein at their desire '.[1] This is only an example which might be repeated over and over again. Thus we may read that on August 21, 1419. 'came good men of the mistery of Linenwevers and presented to the Mayor and Aldermen certain articles for the government of their mystery,' the second of which is—

That members of the mistery sell only good and serviceable estuff under penalty prescribed.[2]

Sometimes the touch of grim humour comes into the doings of these Plantagenet men. Among the records is an entry of November 11, 1364, relating how

[1] Riley, *Memorials of London Life*, 322
[2] _____

John Rightways and John Penrose, taverners, were charged with trespass in the tavern of Walter Daget in Eastchepe, on the eve of St. Martin, and there selling unsound and unwholesome wines, to the deceit of the common people, the contempt of the King, to the shameful disgrace of the officers of the City and to the grievous damage of the commonalty. John Ryghtways was discharged and John Penrose found guilty; he was to be imprisoned a year and a day, to drink a draught of the bad wine, and the rest to be poured over his head, and to forswear the calling of a vintner in the City of London for ever.

This is the kind of work for which the Plantagenet men of London stood. It tells of their character, strong, virile, and honest. City records have preserved to us such photographs of city life as each student may be able to draw from them. They are intensely human in all respects, and in their company we seem to be rubbing up against veritable flesh and blood. The Plantagenet Londoner is a man worth knowing. He comes to us all too dimly from his remote past, but he is definitely a personality, and a great one withal.

One would not grudge to these men one atom of the credit that is due to them from us of this age. But Plantagenet London possessed a greater citizen than all of them a greater citizen than most other mediaeval cities can boast of. I mean, of course, Geoffrey Chaucer. Chaucer, Shakespeare, Milton are world-names from London. Among the members of the Vintners' Company were the father and grandfather of Geoffrey Chaucer His early home was in Thames Street near where the South-Eastern Railway crosses, and here, no doubt, in his boyhood, Geoffrey on many occasions assist'd his f-th-- in h-- wine t-p helping to fill up the citizens' wine-pots, helping on the dreams, we may be quite sure, which ended in his giving from his London home his great world-poem. Is there anything quite so beautiful as Chaucer's calmness in the description of the Southwark Inn, where he conceived the story of the Canterbury pilgrims —

> Byfel that, in that sesoun on a day,
> In Southwerk at the Tabbard as I lay,
> Redy to wenden on my pilgrimage
> To Canturbury with ful devout corage.
> At night was come into that hostelrie
> Wel nyne and twenty in a companye,
> Of sundry folk, by adventure i-falle
> In felaschipe, and pilgryms were thei alle,
> That toward Canturbury wolden ryde
> The chambres and the stables weren wyde,
> And wel we weren esud atte beste.
> And schortly, whan the sonne was to reste,
> So hadde I spoken with hem everychon,
> That I was of here felawschipe anon,
> And made forward erly to aryse,
> To take oure weye thei as I yow devyse
> But natheles, whiles I have tyme and space,
> Or that I ferthere is this tale pace,
> Me thinketh it accordant to resoun,
> To telle yow alle the condicioun
> Of eche of hem so as it semed me,
> And which they weren, and of what degre,
> And eek in what array that they were inne

John Gower, the great friend of Chaucer, 'my disciple and my poete,' as he calls him, lies buried in St Saviour's Church. His monument is one of the best mementoes of this great period, for it tells of the peace beneath the fury, a peace under which poetry could be written and friendships formed showing of what I.......   .   .   ''   W   '   .   such

monuments left. If the old churches had remained to us we should indeed have had a goodly list of London names to record. They are preserved in the simplest form by a print of 1668, the title of which I will quote as an indication of what it can add to our historical information : 'The catalogue of most of the memorable Tombes Grave stones, Plates, Escutcheons or Atchievements in the demolisht or yet extant churches of London from St. Katharine beyond the Tower to Temple Barre, the out-parishes being included, a work of great weight and consequently to be indulged and countenanced by such who are gratefully ambitious of preserving the memory of their ancestors By P. Fisher, sometime Serjant-Major of Foot. London: printed Anno MDCLXVIII.' These, however are names only, though they are true London names.

CHAPTER XVIII

LONDON AS THE NATIONAL CITY

IN all that we have hitherto discovered of the history of London we have seen it as a struggling London— struggling against Anglo-Saxon, against Norman, against Plantagenet. And this fact is the most significant element in her history. The necessity for the struggle takes us right back to her origin as a city of the Roman empire left in Britain without the sovereignty of Rome but with all the traditions and the vitality of her Roman origin and life. She came through Anglo-Saxon tribalism on this basis. She was claimed by the great Ælfred in his struggle against the Northmen on this basis. She struggled against the magnificent governing forces of Norman and Plantagenet on this basis, and finally she passed from the position of a city in an unformed state to the position of an institution belonging to and becoming an essential part of a gradually formed state. The building up of the state was the work of the Plantagenets. It meant the destruction of the city's independence, but it also meant its entrance into the great work of nation building. Looking back over the centuries, nothing is more remarkable in municipal history than the gradual change in the relationship of London to the state. The struggle was fierce, but the city comes out

of it strongly and well, accepting her new position
with a self-consciousness which reveals a political
insight of extraordinary force and instinct, and working through that position with a power that helped
state development more than any other political or
sovereign influence in the country.   For indeed,
strenuous as it was, the fight for rights and privileges
was never a factious fight.   It went straight to the
point at issue, and when, as was generally the case,
new views were revealed during the fight, the city
took up its rights and privileges with the new views
attached to them.   It is in this way that the great
political insight of the municipal leaders of Plantagenet
times stands out.   The city would not bear easily
encroachment by the Crown, but it never disputed the
political pre-eminence of the Crown.   It would not
put up with the personal tyranny of the monarch,
or of a noble, but it used its conquests over these
only to regain what had been lost, not to establish
fresh and inconsequential rights.   It controlled its
own citizens when state law left them entirely alone,
but it would not allow its citizens to be imposed upon
by other cities at home or abroad, or by town or country
magnates.   The period was one of struggle, and the
ebb and flow of the movement were very strong;
but all through the various struggles constitutional
development was never put out of gear; it was allowed
to work its way through bloodshed and disaster,
tyranny and oppression, all the terrible evils of
mediaeval times, and come out clean at the end.

When we inquire, as we should inquire, how London
has borne herself, imperial city of the British people,
the answer is clear and decisive—she has played a great

and a patriotic part, revealing at times her ancient
independence of English life, and the unconscious
continuance of this spirit during the later ages, but
always, except on one miserable occasion, to be mentioned later on taking her stand for liberty and right
I cannot go through all the details of proof for this
statement, but I can point out the great pausing places
where events, having strained the constitutional
machinery, have revealed thereby some of the most
interesting features of that constitution.

We have already seen how English London stood
by the growing English state and, accepting the
sovereignty of the accepted kings, how she worked
loyally to the end   Her support of Ælfred, Eadward,
and Athelstan is represented by her resistance always
to the northern enemies   Her support even of the
unworthy Æthelred was strenuous and consistent.
Her support of the gallant and unfortunate Eadmund
Ironside was a great effort.   Her support of Cnut was
the support of a monarch whom the nation had
accepted, just as her ultimate support of William was.
Perhaps her support of Henry I and of Stephen was
strained in the direction of faction.   Her opposition to
John was on the old lines, but her support of Henry IV,
of Edward IV, and of Richard III was again the
straining of her institutional independence to obtain
a particular political result.   But in whatever form
support was given, the main fact for consideration is
that it was given, that it was accepted, that it was
looked upon as national and proper, or, at all events,
as constitutional.   And this makes the position of
London unique among the cities of Britain.   It was
not a mere military support shut her had to against

a claimant for the throne in favour of another claimant,
or as Bristol shut her gates against Charles   It was
a constitutional support, accepting or assisting a
monarch whose claim had appealed to the nation, and
acting in this form by direct participation in the
constitutional theory of election to the throne, which
has always been associated with the English sovereignty.
That this position comes to Plantagenet London through
Anglo-Saxon times is significant of its origin in pre-
Saxon times, for nothing in Anglo-Saxon history gives
credence to the idea that so profound a doctrine could
have originated in the Anglo-Saxon conception of the
burgh or the city, or of the state.   No other city lays
claim to it except London.   There is something
approaching it in the manner in which the Devonshire
city treated William, but there is no continuance
of such a position, even with Exeter.   And thus we
are able to state with unmistakable clearness that
the constitutional relations of London with Norman
and Plantagenet sovereigns places her apart from all
the other cities of Britain, and gives to her history
a position which has to be explained by reference to
other conditions than those which obtained in her later
history.   How closely these events are connected with
modern times is illustrated by the fact that when King
George V proceeded to the city after his coronation
at Westminster, he followed the traditional practice,
as King Edward VII and Queen Victoria, sovereigns
of the present era, followed it before him, of asking
for admission into the city at the Bar of the City—the
sovereign asking for admission to his capital city !
This was formerly done at Ludgate, the most ancient
of the city gates, and was no mere ceremonial kept up

as a picturesque survival. It was next transferred to the Bar at the extra-mural boundary of the city; finally it is carried out at the site of the old Bar, and has become, of course, a mere ceremony. But in these two connected ceremonies, coronation at Westminster and admission to the city, we have the last remnants of the ancient constitutional position of London—the monarch elected in English fashion outside the city, and then being admitted within the city in London fashion. The quasi-independence of London could not be better illustrated. It comes to her from her Roman past. It shows that it was the same system of government passing on from Roman to Norman times, not a different system altogether. It dominates her present conception of necessary aloofness from the developed London which surrounds her. It is a factor in modern politics.

The story of London as the national city is therefore a double one, and down to the end of the Plantagenet period this duality is shown in a marked degree. After this period we have change. London was first of all pre-eminent as a constitutional unit. She was destined to be equally pre-eminent as a commercial unit. The Tudor sovereignty brought with it, or was accompanied by, a new order of things. This new order was the triumph of the commercial ideal as distinct from the old communal ideal. Ugly moments arose, as we have seen, when London was communal London. Still more ugly moments arose, as we shall see presently, when individualism reared its head uncontrolled. Through it all London has kept many of her old traditions of city greatness—in a sense she keeps them still, but they were and are, traditions only, not actual, living, governing forces. They, no doubt, influenced her citizens on great occasions, as we may presently see, but they were not the continuous outcome of the city life, and their absence is the sign of the passing of London to her modern stage.

One instance of the assertion of ancient rights is peculiarly interesting. It relates to the independence of the Tower, which has already been described as a feature of both Norman and Plantagenet London. It reappears in Tudor London. A report to the Queen upon the state of the Tower of London, 1597, states that 'the Citye of London did and doth pretend Tythe unto your Mati. soil of Tower Hill and Est Smythfeilde even unto the ditch of the Tower', and in 1599 a formal document was prepared of 'Argumentes and Recordes to proove that the Towre of London and the libertyes thereunto belonging doth not lye within the cownty of the cittie of London'.[1] This is the Norman and Plantagenet position put into legal form. In the earlier period the contentions of the city were carried out by the citizens themselves In Tudor times they were carried out at the law courts, the same ancient rights but not the same method of expressing or defending them.

This passing from ancient to modern conditions means a deliberate and conscious deflection from the past. Tudor London was definitely not the old communal city of Plantagenet times She was not so independent municipally, because her citizens were aiming at commercial success, which meant to them individual wealth, and few things are more interesting than the note which comes to the historian from the

transition period of the Tudors.   The London of the
Tudors, great city that she was, had become absorbed
by the state.   She was no longer the unique great city
helping to build up the state.   She was a great city
still, but she was only the greatest of several great
cities.   She was subordinate to the sovereign monarch
in a peculiar fashion, not in the Plantagenet fashion.
She helped the state on specially great occasions, but
no longer as a contributor to state institutions on all
occasions.   In a word, London had entered the final
stages of her evolution, and Tudor London was modern
London in all essentials

This may be illustrated by one impressive event.
The Saxon settlements all round London had left
Tudor London settled amidst open fields.   But Tudor
London did not want ancient systems of agriculture at
her gates, and so she set about enclosures.   Stow gives
us a picture of what was happening in his own day,
which will best tell the story to us.   At Houndsditch,
he says, 'was a fair field,' which, ' as all other about
the city, was inclosed, reserving open passage there-
into for such as were disposed.'   And then he goes on
to say :—

And now concerning the inclosures of common
grounds about this cittie whereof I mind not much to
argue.   Edwarde Hall setteth downe a note of his time,
to wit. in the 5th or 6th of Henry VIII.   Before this
time, sayth hee, the inhabitantes of the townes aboute
London, as Iseldone, Hoxton, Shorsditch and others,
had so inclosed the common fieldes with hedges and
ditches, that neyther the yong men of the city might
shoote, nor the auncient persons walke for theyr
pleasures in those fieldes ; but that either their bowes
and ai   ⟨illegible⟩   ouest

persons arrested or indighted, saying that no Londoner ought to goe out of the city, but in the highwaies. This saying so grieued the Londoners, that suddainlie this yeare a great number of the citie assembled themselues in a morning, and a turner in a fooles coate came crying through the citty, ' Shouels and spades!—shouels and spades!' So many of the people followed, that it was a wonder to behold ; and within a short space all the hedges about the city were cast down, and the diches filled vp and euerything made plaine, such was the diligence of these workmen. (Edit. Kingsford ii. 77.)

There was very little difference in the Stuart period. Stuart London was Tudor London more developed along modern political lines. It was the statesmen and politicians of the nation, not the influence of London, which, more than anything else, decided the destinies of England during the stress of civil war, during the commonwealth period, and during the revolution period of Jacobean times. London fell into line, but she did not lead in the older sense—in the manner that she led under the Plantagenets. That she took the popular side was all to the good of the nation, but she was only one element of the popular side. The state had become the only dominant force, and the great city had to take her place amongst the institutions which had evolved from a great historic past.

We may, perhaps, indicate some of the greatest moments of these later times. Amidst the clash and struggle of them there are episodes which show the city standing in her old way as the guardian of English liberty and English tradition of constitutional freedom. She stood loyally by the great Tudor soveroign when the Spaniard was threatening the

independence of England, and hastened to respond
to that noble appeal addressed from Tilbury by Queen
Elizabeth to 'my loving people'—a state document
which ought to be set up in all our schools as a model
of beautiful English language and of loyal princedom:
'I know I have but the body of a weak and feeble
woman; but I have the heart of a king, and a king of
England too'. These are the noblest words ever recorded of an English sovereign, and they were spoken
from one of the defences of London

Another great moment was when, in the latter half
of the reign of Queen Elizabeth, the London merchants,
wealthy, prosperous, and enterprising, began to look
with longing eyes towards the wonderful 'Indies',
whose treasures had hitherto been brought to them by
other nations, or captured from the rich carracks bound
for Portugal or Spain. During the last twenty years
of the Queen's reign several small expeditions were
sent out, some of which obtained rich booty, though
with terrible loss of life   In 1599 an association of
London merchants was formed, and amongst the
names of these 'Adventurers' to the East Indies are
found representatives of each of the twelve great City
Companies except the Fishmongers; representatives,
too, of almost all the great mercantile families who
played so great a part in the history of London during
the seventeenth century   Preparations for a voyage
were begun; four ships—the *Red Dragon*, *Hector*,
Ascension, and *Susan*—were made ready, Captain
James Lancaster being appointed 'General of the
Fleet', and Captain John Davis (of North-West
Passage fame) his second in command.   Hakluyt,
their historiographer was frequently consulted   d on

the last day of December, 1600, the royal sanction for
which they were waiting was bestowed, when Queen
Elizabeth signed the first charter of the East India
Company, and Captain Lancaster sailed from Woolwich
in February, 1601   A General Court of the East
India Company was held on the 16th of June, 1603,
and the following minute occurs :—

The Assention retourned from the East Indies.

Ther is propounded to this genneralyty the choice
of a convenient place of receipte of the goodes retorned
in the Assontion, which is nowe come in to the Ryver,
and for ther better Direction what places are likelie to
be heird for that purpose, ther is nominated thes
severall places or houses hereafter following, out of
which the Committees may make ther choice uppon
the viewe of the fittest.

Warehouses

        The Vault under the exchange
        Sr. John Spencers Warehouse.
        The great house in Sething Lane
        Sr. Edward Osbornes house
        The La. Barnes her house
        Mr. Cartwrights house

Men to attende on baorde.

London was beautified by Tudor architects in a way
that only Tudor architects could beautify a city.   Buildings that have been destroyed by the ruthless hand of
modern iconoclasm have yielded art treasures in the
shape of architectural mouldings which our schools and
museums are only too willing to exhibit, as for instance
at Suffolk House, in Southwark, the residence of Charles
Brandon, Duke of Suffolk.   But the greatest efforts
were at Whitehall   Wolsey's palace, York House, was
delivered to the king by charter, 21 Henry VIII, and
was then renamed Whitehall   With its front towards

the Thames, and another towards St James's Park, its
gateways, Holbein Gate as the north entrance and
King's Gate as the southern, it must have been an
architectural glory   The palace was destroyed by fire
in January, 1697, and the Holbein Gateway was pulled
down in 1759 to make way for the present Parliament
Street, one of those instances of senseless destruction,
instead of useful adaptation, which make those of us
who care for the beautiful feel so hopeless.   There is
not much of Whitehall left now.   The Banqueting
House designed by Inigo Jones is the only complete
building, but parts of the offices of the Board of Trade
and of the Treasury, mostly underground, are structural
remains of the old palace and reveal many beautiful
features   In the meantime the Tudor addition to
Westminster Abbey, Henry VII's chapel, will illustrate how grandly the architecture of the period was
ushering in the greatness of extended London.

A very recent destruction has taken away a
characteristic bit of Stuart London, Spring Gardens.
This place is now an entrance into St. James's
Park, and it was formerly a garden attached to the
King's Palace at Westminster, with a bowling-green,
butts, bathing pond, and pheasant yard.   It derived
its name from a jet or spring of water   It was apparently included within the Royal Park of St. James.
Thus, in a letter in the Verney Collection, dated
10th December, 1677, it is stated that an arrest was
made within the privilege of St. James's Park in Old
Spring Garden.   This is confirmed by a news letter,
dated 15th December, 1693, where it is reported that
the Spanish Ambassador was lodged at Spring Garden
and com̄... ... d t̄ ... l... ... P... ... C... b... C... pel

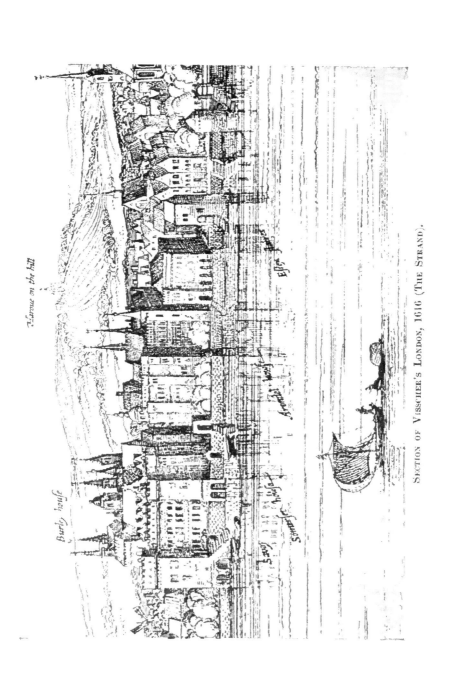

Harrow on the hill

Burly house

Essex...

...house

Somer...

SECTION OF VISSCHER'S LONDON, 1616 (THE STRAND).

there, but was stopped by the principal officers of Whitehall because 'c'est un lieu privilegié dans l'enclos de Witehall.' Until quite recently the Queen's taxes due by tenants in Spring Gardens were collected by the Board of Green Cloth at Buckingham Palace, their district being the precincts of the Palace. The topography of the place is noticed in a letter from Rushworth, the historian, to Lord Fairfax, dated 20th December, 1645, in which the following passage occurs.—

There is a house att Charinge Crosse next doore to my Ladye Fairfaxes to bee lett about a moneth hence. It is I heare about forty pounds a yeare, hath a back door into Spring Garden and a convenient house' (*Hist. MSS. Com*, ix 438).

In 1634 it appears to have been more or less a place of fashionable resort, and therefore, it is presumed, to some extent detached from the King's Palace. Lord Digby was apprehended for striking Will Crofts in Spring Garden, and he answered 'that he took it for a common bowling place where all paid money for their coming in' (*Strafford Papers*, i. 262). In 1649 Evelyn records in his *Diary* that he 'treated ladies of my relations in Spring Garden' Evidence as to the character of Spring Gardens as a resort for pleasure seekers is indirectly given in a letter from Lord Yarmouth to his wife, 21st July, 1676, wherein it is stated that in the garden at Lord Howard's 'the walks were as full as Spring Garden, and in I went and saw dancing on the bowling-green by torchlight' (*Hist. MSS. Com*, vii. 532). In 1662 Pepys and his two maids 'gathered pinks' in the Garden, but a little after this period the ground was built upon and the 'New

Spring Garden ', as it came to be called, was opened at Lambeth, where it was afterwards known as the celebrated Vauxhall Gardens. The ground so built upon is called in the rate books of St Martin's the 'Inner Spring Garden' and the 'Outer Spring Garden '.

Passing on from these details which reflect the great epoch of Shakespeare's life in London, we resume the main narrative of modern London. There was one specially significant intervening period when London once more resumed her old functions, and in the old fashion was once more a communal city. This was during the period of the commonwealth. Let me illustrate this point by enumerating the London regiments which accompanied Essex to the great fight at Newbury. They mustered in Finsbury fields in September, 1643, and consisted of the white, yellow, orange, blue, red, and green regiments, the Tower Hamlets, the Southwark, and the Westminster regiments. But though in this enumeration we lose touch with the citizen soldiers marshalled from the wards of the ancient city, we pick it up again when we ascertain that all the regiments except one were commanded by the aldermen. This is most significant. It carries on the older tradition, of which we have seen the earliest example in Ansgar, the great sheriff who commanded the Londoners at Hastings, and it may well be that we have something more than tradition, an actual reverting to ancient practice, when the independence of the city was emphasized by the existence of her citizen army, organized and commanded in the ancient communal fashion.

Trade was still the dominating feature, however, and

it is interesting to see how the topography of London was altered to suit its commercial necessities. For further convenience to trade the statute of 22 Charles II, cap 11, enacted that 'the channel of Bridewell Dock from the Thames to Holborn Bridge shall be sunk to a sufficient level whereby to make it navigable'. In breadth this channel and the wharves on each side were not to be less than 100 or more than 120 feet, and the lines and levels were to be set out by the Lord Mayor and aldermen within a given time, subject to his Majesty's approval. All costs were to be defrayed by the corporation out of the coal duty (s. 42), and they were to charge reasonable rates for use of the navigation and quays   This channel was accordingly made and levelled pursuant to the Act, but in 1732 that part of it lying between Fleet Bridge (at the end of Fleet Street) and Holborn Bridge was found by experience to be of no benefit to trade ; the navigation was disused and choked by mud ; and it had been for several years previously 'a grievous and dangerous nuisance' (Recital to 6 Geo. II, c. 22).   An Act of 1732, therefore, enabled the corporation to fill up that part of the channel lying between these two bridges, and vested the fee simple of the ground in them to such uses and purposes as they and their successors shall think proper and convenient for the benefit and advantage of the city' (6 Geo. II, c. 22, s. 2 ; and see 29 Geo. II, c. 86, s. 24).[1]

I must now mention the period—the one period—of real degradation. Of course it belongs to the degradation period of English history, that of the

---

[1] Clifford's *History of Private Bill Legislation* vol. ii. p. 629

Restoration. 'I was present,' says John Evelyn in his
Diary (June 18, 1683),

and heard the humble submission and petition of the
Lord Maior Sheriffs and Aldermen on behalf of the
citty of London, on the quo warranto against their
charter which they delivered to his Majesty in the
Presence Chamber. It was delivered kneeling and
then the King and Council went into the Council
Chamber the Maior and his brethren attending still
in the Presence Chamber. After a short space they
were called in, and my Lord Keeper made a speech to
them exaggerating the disorderly and riotous behaviour
in the late election and polling for Papellon and Du
Blois after the Common Hall had been formally dissolved; with other misdemeanours, libells on the
government etc.; by which they had incurred His
Majesty's high displeasure and that but for their
submission and such articles as the King should
require their obedience to he would certainly enter
judgement against them which hitherto he had sus-
pended. The things required were as follows. that
they should neither elect Maior Sheriff Alderman
Recorder Common Serjeant Town Clerk Coroner or
Steward of Southwark without his Majesty's appro-
bation, and that if they presented any his Majesty did
not like they should proceed in wonted manner to a
second choice, if that was disapproved his Majesty to
nominate them and if within three daies they thought
good to assent to this all former miscarriages should
be forgotten.

This, then, is the end of the city's great independence,
an independence which helped it to build the state as
it evolved the English conception of a city. John
Evelyn's bitter remark, 'And so they tamely parted
with their so ancient privileges after they had dined
and been treated by the King,' is a miserable record,

but it has to be told to those who would understand the unfolding of London.

If it is thought that I have paid too much attention to the earliest history of London, it must be remembered that it is the earliest history which has dominated the later.   Later London in Plantagenet times would not have been able to act as she did if it had not been for earlier London.   Tudor London, even with its entirely new aspect, would have taken a different place among the great cities of Britain if her Plantagenet history had been different.   The disgrace of late Stuart London would not have been so marked if all that had gone before had not been so great.   Even modern London would have been different.   If it is true that the rising street from Fleet Street to St. Paul's, still preserving its history in its name of Ludgate Hill, is the site of the earth ramparts up which Caesar's soldiers marched to conquer the Celtic stronghold. if we worship Christianwise in St. Paul's Cathedral on the very site where our Celtic ancestors worshipped paganwise, if almost every spot upon which we step is historic ground which tells us something of the evolution stages of London—we cannot refuse to acknowledge that the understanding of ancient is the necessary step to the understanding of modern London.

I think the facts that have been noted are remarkable facts in the history of a city.   They betoken a continuity of interests which cannot be misunderstood, and they carry forward the position of London as the one city in all Britain which, having received its independence in the constitution of Rome. used its independence in the constitution of Britain.

CHAPTER XIX

TUDOR AND STUART LONDON CHANGES

WE have noted the great architectural results of Tudor London and indicated that they reflected the new glories of London. They were, however, not the only aspect of London, for its new glories were accompanied by sadder things.

These were the beginnings of modern life—those items of modern life which tell not of the citizenship of London, but of the irresponsible acts of congregated individualism and all its unnamed results. It will be well to refer to this new aspect of London under the Tudors and the Stuarts, as it draws the contrast with what has gone before so very strongly. For this purpose I shall have to rely upon quotations from contemporary literature the evidence from which has not yet been collected and used. I shall pick my way among pamphlets and rhymes, satires and songs, to try in the shortest way to give a picture of some sort, a picture—not of course complete, but not altogether out of focus, I hope—of the conditions of London under the Tudors and Stuarts after it had thrown off the communal shell and had started on its free commercialism as a national city.

That the buildings of London were not all of a picturesque type we may gather from many sources One of the earliest dates from the early years of

James the First which details the causes and results of the continuous building, and will appeal to the reader if it is given in its original quaint wording.

The desire of Profitte greatly increaseth Buyldinges, and so muche the more, for that this greate Concurse of all sortes of people draweinge here vnto the Cittie everie man seeketh out places, highe-wayes, lanes, and coverte corners to buylde upon, yf it be but Sheddes, Cottages, and small Tenementes for people to lodge inn, wch have not any meanes either to lyve or to imploye themselves aboute any other maner of thinge, then either to begge or steale, by wch meanes of Idelnes it cometh to passe that in some one parrishe, there are above two thowsand people wch doe receive releife, and many thowsandes wch doe lyve w^thout any man's knowledge howe, not vseinge any manner of Arte or Trade. Thes sorte of coveteous Buylders exacte great renttes, and daiely doe increase them, in so muche that a poore handie craftesman is not able by his paynefull laboure to paye the rentte of a smale Tenement and feede his ffamilie. Thes Buylders neither regarde the good of the Comon-wealthe the preservacon of the health of the Cittie, the maynetenance of honeste Tradesmen, neither doe they regarde of what base condicion soever their Tenantes are, or what lewde and wycked practizes soever they vse so as their exacted renttes be duely payed, the wch for the moste parte they doe receave either weekely or moonthely.

The third sorte of Buylders are suche as doe buylde for pleasure here vnto the Cittie, and for the most parte thes Buyldinges were either erected by great persons, or by providente Gentillmen of the Countrey, either to save Charge of hospitalitie, or for some other their private vse and pleasure, when they shall at any tyme have occasion to repayre vnto the Cittie, or they are buylte by rytche Citizens in Gardens, and other convenient places here vnto the Cittie, the better to recreate themselves in the Sommer time, &c. Thes

sortes of Buyldinges were erected for private and
necessarie vses by the parties that fyrste buylte them;
but when as by deathe or otherwise they parted from
them, and that they came to the handes of such who
either for necessitie or Coveteousnes devided them
and rented them out, then presently after there doth
enter and dwelle in them, either those sorte of lewde
people wch are before-meencioned, or a worser sorte
then they, wch are Papistes, who in thes places of
couert doe shrowde themselves in suche sorte, as when
they canot hyde themselves in any parte of the lande
else where but they shall be espied, yet here they can
shrowde themselves in some devided place or garden-
howse, and doe ther both vse their supersticious
service, (drawinge many of the weaker sorte of his
Maties subjects vnto their false worshipp of the true
God, and also doe there plotte all their trecheries and
wycked attempts whatsoever, bothe againste the king's
Maiestie the State, and their own Countrie.)

This was an echo from the old London of the
Plantagenets. Its cry was met by legislative action.
Everyone knows the mad attempt of Queen Elizabeth
to restrict the building of houses beyond the area to
which it had reached in her days, and her successors
on the throne followed her policy, but equally without
avail. The Act of Elizabeth passed in 1580, but that
it failed of its purpose there can be little doubt, for on
the 22nd of June, 1602, another proclamation was
issued, with more stringent provisions. It directs that
houses built in defiance of previous Acts and proclama-
tions should be pulled down, and the timber given to
the poor of the parish in which the offence was committed. All shops and sheds built in the seven years
past are to be pulled down, and tenements divided into
several habitations are to have their inmates turned

out, and offenders to be made answerable to the Star
Chamber. This was one of the last Acts of Elizabeth's
reign. but her successor, King James, on July 11, the
following year, issued a proclamation to the same effect
It was a season of infection, and it complains that one
of the 'chiefest occasions of the great plague and
mortality' was caused by 'idle, indigent, and dissolute
persons', and the 'pestering of them in small and strait
rooms' Like all the others, this appears to have been
ineffectual, for only four years afterwards, on October 12, 1607, another appeared, declaring emphatically
that unless by special licence 'there shalbe *no more
new buildings* in or neere the sayde city of London'.
It is remarkable, however, that 'two miles of the citie
gates' is the limit specified, which is one mile less
than in previous edicts, the other provisions are much
the same as those which formerly appeared The value
of this authoritative declaration is shown in the succeeding year in another proclamation, dated July 25,
1608, complaining of the evasions through the 'neglect
of officers and justices' and the 'covetous desire of
gain'. Seven years now pass over before we hear of
any more attempts by authority to arrest the inevitable
law of progress. But in 1615 a proclamation, dated
July 16, appeared, which in its composition is remarkable, and was doubtless by the hand of James himself.
It says, 'Our citie of London is become the greatest, or
next the greatest citie of the Christian world; it is
more than time that there be an *utter cessation* of
further new building' 'This', it says, 'shalbe the
furthest and utmost period and end of them.' It com-
mends the recent paving of Smithfield, bringing the
new stream into the west part of the city and suburbs,

the pesthouse, Sutton's hospital. Britaine's Burse, the re-edifying of Aldgate, Hicks' Hall, &c., but it speaks in great determination of putting a stop to further increase, and no one is to expect licences again. Exactly fifteen years now pass away in silence, when we find Charles I. on July 16, 1630, issuing a proclamation to the same intent as those that went before it. Even under the protectorate they did not cease to endeavour to repress, by the same vain and ineffectual efforts, the expanse of the city into the green fields beyond it.[1]

It is worth while quoting Queen Elizabeth's proclamation against new buildings in and about London, as it contains matter of much constitutional interest.

The Queenes Majestic perceiving the state of the citie of London (being aunciently termed her chambre) and the subuibes and confines thereof to increase dayly, by accesse of people to inhabite in the same, in such ample sort, as thereby many inconveniences are seene already, but many greater of necessity like to followe, being such as her majestie cannot neglect to remedie, having the principal care, under Almightie God, to foresee aforehand, to have her people in such a citie and confines not onlie well-governed by ordinarie justice, to serve God and obey her majestie, (which, by reason of such multitudes lately increased, can hardly be done without devise of more new jurisdictions and officers for that purpose) but to be also provided of sustentation of victual, foode, and other like necessaries for man's life, upon reasonable prices, without which no citie can long continue.

And finally, to the preservation of her people in health, which may seem impossible to continue, though presently, by God's goodness, the same is perceived to be in better estate universally, than hath been in man's memorie ; yet where there are such great multitudes

of people brought to inhabite in small roomes, whereof
a great part are scene very poore, yea, such as must
live of begging, or by worse meanes, and they heaped
up together, and in a sort smothered with many families
of children and servantes in one house or small tenement; it must needes followe, if any plague or popular
sickness should, by God's permission, enter amongst
those multitudes, that the same would not only spread
itself, and invade the whole citie and confines, but that
a great mortalitie would ensue the same, where her
majesties personal presence is many times required;
besides the great confluence of people from all parts of
the realme, by reason of the ordinary termes of justice
there holden, the infection would be also dispersed
through all other partes of the realme, to the manifest
danger of the whole body thereof; out of the which
neither her majesties own person can be (but of God's
special ordinance) exempted, nor any other, whatsoever
they be.

For remedie whereof, as time may now serve, until
by some further good order, be had in parliament or
otherwise, the same may be remedied, her majestie,
by good and deliberate advise of her counsell, and
being also thereto moved by the considerate opinions
of the lorde-mayor, aldermen. and other the grave wise
men in and about the citie, doth charge and straightly
command all manner of persons, of what qualitie soever
they be, to desist and forbeare from any new buildings
of any house or tenement within three miles from any
of the gates of the said citie of London, to serve for
habitation or lodging for any person, where no former
house hath bene knowen to have been in the memorie
of such as are now living, and also to forbeare from
letting or setting, or suffering any more families then
one onely to be placed or to inhabite from henceforth
in any one house that heretofore hath bene inhabited.

And to the intent this her majesties royal command-
ment and necessary provision may take place, and be
duely observed, for so universal a benefite to the whole

body of the realme, for whose respects all particular
persons are bound, by God's lawe and man's to forbear
from their particular and extraordinarie lucre; her
majestie straightly chargeth the lorde-mayor of the
citie of London, and all other officers having authoritie
in the same, and also all justices of peace, lordes and
bailifes of liberties not being within the jurisdiction of
the said lorde-mayor of London, to foresee, that no
person do begin to prepare any foundation for any new
house, tenement, or building, to serve to receive or
hold any inhabitants to dwell or lodge, or to use any
victualling therein, where no former habitation hath
bene in the memorie of such as now do live: but that
they be prohibited and restrained so to do. And both
the persons that shall so attempt to the contrary, and
all manner of workmen that shall (after warning given)
continue in any such work tending to such newe buildings, to be committed to close prison, and there to
remain without baile, until they find good sureties,
with bonds for reasonable sums of money (to be
forfeitable and recoverable at her majesties suite, for
the use of the hospitals in and about the said city) that
they will not at any time hereafter attempt the like.

And further the said officers shall seaze all manner
of stuff, so (after warning given) brought to the place
where such newe buildings shall be intended, and the
same cause to be converted and employed in any
publick use for the city or parish where the same shall
be attempted.

And for the avoyding of the multitudes of families
heaped up in one dwelling-house, or for the converting
of any one house into a multitude of such tenements
for dwelling or victualling-places, the said lorde-mayor,
and all other officers, in their several liberties within
the limits of three miles, as above mentioned, shall
commit any person giving cause of offence. from the
day of the publication of this present proclamation, to
close prison, as is afore limited.

And also for the offences in this part of increase of

many indwellers, or. as they be commonly termed. inmates or underfitters, which have been suffered within these seven years. contrary to the good auncient laws or customes of the City, or of the boroughes and parishes within the foresaid limit of three miles afore-mentioned. the said lorde-mayor, and the other officers above-mentioned, shall speedily cause to be redressed in their ordinarie courtes and law dayes, betwixt this and the feast of All-Saintes next coming, within which times such underfitters or inmates may provide themselves other places abroade in the realme, where many houses rest uninhabited, to the decay of divers auncient boroughes and townes. And, because her majestie intendeth to have this ordinance duely executed, her pleasure is, that the said lorde-mayor of London and other the officers, having jurisdiction within the said space of three miles above-mentioned, shall, after the proclamation hereof, as speedily as they may, meete in some convenient place near to the said city, and there (after conference had) accord among themselves how to proceed to the execution hereof: and if any cause shall so require, to imparte to her majesties privy counsell. any let or impediment that may arise, to the intent that remedy be given to any such impediment, according to her majesties pleasure heretofore expressed.

Given at Nonesuch. the seventh day of July, 1580, in the two-and-twentieth year of her majesties reign.

Two things will be noticed here. First, that it is the sovereign and not the city who legislates in the matter of city buildings, a change from the more ancient system which illustrates the altered position of the city in relation to the state. Secondly, that the Lord Mayor and aldermen of the city are associated in this decree of the sovereign relating to events and circumstances beyond the boundaries of the Lord Mayor's jurisdiction. Here was a moment when

London might have grown greater by extending her boundaries. But there was the old shrinking back, the old desire to keep separate the city and its external surroundings. The city would be jealous of extending London, but would not help it.

London awoke to a unique greatness when she so quietly housed Shakespeare in her midst and admitted him to an understanding of her life, the reflection of which has helped to produce one of the world poems. Shakespeare was a Londoner in a very special sense. All his experience came from there. Court, noble, merchant, travellers, sailors from all the world over; scenes of revelry by night and of great doings by day, scenes in the city houses and streets and by the dock landing stages, in the courts of law and in the merchants' markets and exchanges, in the churches and the schools, in the playing fields and along the walks to Islington and Camberwell,—all these were contributors to the storehouse of knowledge acquired to produce the great results that all the world now acclaims In particular, the interest which London took in the Armada attack, fight, and victory must have been enormous, and Mr. Fairman Ordish has very ably pictured for us the influence it had in shaping some of Shakespeare's scenes.[1] Mr. Ernest Law has recently shown that more than a hundred performances of his plays took place at Whitehall under the patronage of Queen Elizabeth and to a less extent under that of James the First.

We may get behind the scenes that Shakespeare saw by reference to contemporary tracts which were published so frequently, and it would be well for one

---

[1] *Shakespeare's London* 193-7.

moment to dwell upon this We can see the citizens
pouring forth from the gates into the fields beyond.
In a poem written *circa* 1576, entitled *A warning to
London by the fall of Antwerp*,[1] by Rafe Norris, we see
by one of the allusions that the walls of London were
looked upon as important elements in the city's
safety—

Keep sure thy trench, prepare thy shot.

And again—

Erect your walles, give out your charge

Londoners made the fields beyond their constant
place of resort. In a ballad, *temp* Elizabeth published
by the Percy Society (vol. i.), and entitled *A proper
new balade expressyng the fames concernyng a warnyng
to all London dames*, by Stephen Peell, it says:

And oft when you goe, fayre dames, on a rowe
  In to the feeldes so greene,
You sit and vewe the beautifull hewe
  Of flowres that then be scene

A little later they journeyed out further, and a tract
in the British Museum gives us, both by its title
and its contents, a curious picture of the times in 1699.[2]
It is entitled *A Walk to Islington, with a description of
New Tunbridge Wells and Sadler's Music house* (London, 1699). That Islington was very famous as a
resort for Londoners is to be gathered from the fact
that the Pied Bull Inn there was supposed to have been
Sir Walter Raleigh's country house, and the first place

[1] This is printed by the Percy Society, vol. i.
[2] Pepys records, in 1661, walking in 'Grayes-Inn-Walks, and
thence to Islington, and there eate and drank at the house my father
and we . . . .

in England where tobacco was smoked.   A few verses
of this curious tract may be quoted :

In holiday time, when ladies of London
Walk out with their spouses or think themselves
   undone ;

Then I, like my neighbours to sweeten my life,
Took a walk in the fields.

We sauntered about near the New River head,

We rambled about till we came to a gate
Where abundance of rabble peep'd in at a gate
To gaze at the ladies amidst of their revels.
As fine all as angels, but wicked as devils.

We entred the walks to the rest of the sinners,
Where lime-trees were placed at a regular distance

Some citizens, too, one might easily know
By his formally handing his ' Whither d'ye go ? '
For in the old order you're certain to find 'em
Advance, with their tallow fac'd daughters behind 'em.

Other persons are then described, and the writer
proceeds ·

The sparks that attended to make up the show
Were various, but first we'll begin with the beau,
Whose wig was so bushy, so long, and so fair,
The best part of man was quite covered with hair :
That he looked (as a body might modestly speak it)
Like a calf, with bald face, peeping out of a thicket ;
His locks drudg his coat, which such filthiness harbour,
Tho' made of black cloth, 'tis as white as a barber ;
His sword, I may say, to my best of belief
Was as long as a spit for a sir-loin of beef,
Being graced with a ribbon of scarlet or blue

That hung from the hilt to the heel of his shoe ;
His gate is a strut which he learns from the stage.[1]

The author of this curious tract then goes on to
describe the company to be met, and he does not give
a very flattering account of them. Finally.

When pretty well tired of seeing each novice
Bow down to his idol as if sh' was a goddess,
We walk'd by an outhouse we found had been made
For raffling and lott'ries and such sort of trade,
And, casting an eye into one of the sheds,
Saw a parcel of grave paralitical heads
Sit sipping of coffee and poring on paper.
And some smoaking silently round a wax taper :
Whilst others at gammon, grown peevish with age,
Were wrangling for pen'worths of tea made of sage
In a hovel adjoyning, a cunning sly fox
Stood shov'ling of money down into a box ;
Who by an old project was picking the pockets
Of fools in huge wigs and of jilts in gold lockets ;
Who're strangely bewitch'd to this national evil,
Tho' th' odds that's against 'em would cozen the devil
The Board ev'ry time, I observed, was a winner

The tract then describes the dancing-place, and at last
leads us away to Sadler's Wells, where—

We entered the house, were conducted upstairs,
Where lovers o'er cheesecakes were seated by pairs :

<hr/>

[1] So late as 1736 Islington waters were recommended A letter,
dated April 24, of that year, printed in the fifth report of the Historical
MSS. Commission, says: 'Dr Crowe thinks that if you could abide
cold bathing it would go a great way in your cure He has also
a great opinion of Islington waters for your case' In 1755 was
printed a curious book, entitled *Islington, or, the Humours of the New
Tunbridge Wells* They were apparently first opened about 1684, for
two curious tracts are thus entitled, *A Morning's Ramble, or, Islington
Wells' Burlesq*. 1684, and *An Exclamation from Tunbridge and Epsom against
the new*

The organ and fiddles were scraping and humming,
The guests for more ale on the tables were drumming,
And poor Tom, amaz'd, crying, 'coming, sir, coming.'

The remainder of the description given in this curious
tract is full of interest, though too long to quote now.
From such sources as these can be gained a true
picture of London life in the past.

A curious legend about Moorfields and its origin as
citizen ground is contained in a ballad printed by the
Percy Society (vol. i). It is called *The Life and death
of the two ladies of Finsbury, that gave Moorfields to the
city for the maidens of London to dry cloaths.* A verse
or two describes the events as follows ·

> And likewise when those maidens died
>   They gave those pleasant fields
> Unto our London citizens
>   Which they most bravely build
>
> And now are made most pleasant walks
>   That great contentment yield
>   To maidens of London so fair.
>
> Where lovingly both man and wife
>   May take the evening air,
> And London dames, to dry their cloathes,
>   May hither still repair.

In Richard Johnson's *The Pleasant Walks of Moor-
Fields,* 1607, we have an interesting addition to this
legend. Stow, in 1599, gives some information as to
the improvements going on in his time in Moorfields,[1]
and, says Mr. Collier, ·in the very words which Johnson eight or nine years afterwards repeated : but Stow
did not live to witness, or at all events to record, the

means resorted to by the citizens to complete what
had been so well begun. Stow died on April 5, 1605,
just anterior to the laying-out of the walks and making
the plantations, which are the chief eulogies of Johnson's tracts'[1] Johnson calls Moorfields ' those sweet
and delightfull walks of More fields, as it seemes
a garden to this citty, and a pleasurable place of sweet
ayres for cittizens to walke in'. After relating the
legend that the fields were given to the City in the
time of Edward the Confessor by the daughters of
Sir William Fines, he says, ' these walkes beares the
fashion of a crosse, equelly divided foure wayes, and
likewise squared about with pleasant wals : the trees
thereof makes a gallant show.' There were 291 of
these trees, and ' many of them doe carry proper names
. the first of them at the corner of the middle walke
westward was first of all placed by Sir Leonard Holly-
day, then Lord Maior . . . there standeth neere a tree
called the " two brothers". planted by too little boys,
and sonnes to a citizen here in London '.

I will next give two quotations showing us the house
life of the period on special occasions, although I doubt
not greatly exaggerated in detail.

It is within the memory of man that all the apprentices of Merchants, Lawyers and Mechanicks as well
in London as in other places submitted to the most
servile Employments of the Families that entertain'd
them such as the young gentry, their successors in the
same station scorn so much as the name of now. They
cleaned their own and their masters shoes, brought
water into the houses from the conduits in the streets
which they carried on their shoulders, in long vessels
called tankards ; they waited at table on their masters,

_____
[1] C[...]

wore bands, and had the fore part of their heads
cropped or shorn, according to the method observed at
this time in the Blue Coat hospital. It was the custom
of those days for the master to be followed to Church
on a Sunday by all his household, the Apprentice
arm'd with their bibles and Prayer books closing the
procession, a sight well becoming a Protestant city
(*A Trip through London*).

The following description of citizen life from the
same authority is very curious :—

I am led by the regard which I bear to good company to divert my reader with the history of an enter-
tainment I met with at the house of a citizen in the
ward of Farringdon without, during the late Christmas
holydays.   When I went in, I found the dining room
full of women, to every one of whom I made a profound
bow, and was repaid in a whole circle of courtesies ;
having after some ceremony taken a seat among them,
we had profound silence for near half a minute, notwithstanding the number of females present   For my
part I had fix'd my eyes upon the fire, meditating
what I had best to say: While I was in this study I
could hear one of them whisper to another, *I believe he
thinks we smoak Tobacco*; for my readers must know
I had omitted the city custom, and not kiss'd one of
the ladies   A Hackney Coach stopping at the door,
there issued out of it a smart young fellow in a well
powdered campaign, a suit of superfine cloth, with
a pair of laced ruffles at his wrists · He entered the
room box in hand, offering his snuff to every one of
the company and display'd a fine diamond ring by
keeping his left hand always in motion towards his
forehead ; and began to be inquisitive about the Hour
of the Day to give himself an opportunity of shewing
us his Gold Watch, all of which he perform'd with
awkward dexterity but admirable success, the women
having one and all declar'd themselves in his favour,
by ev ... ... him their ... ... that I ... at for

a cypher or meer mum-chance amongst them. . . . He was instantly followed by a substantial citizen on foot who had trudged it from Tower Hill fenced only with a drab cloak against the inclemency of the weather; neighbour Jobson was now the only guest we waited for and he soon made his appearance . . . in a thick set frock, covered over with silver buttons, a short natural perriwig, the knee bands of his breeches laid with silver, with a silver watch in his pocket almost as large as a pewter porringer, and on his fingers as many gold rings as he had been espoused years to his Help-mate. . . . As soon as we were risen from table . . . the females presently resolved themselves into committees of two or three's all over the dining room, and I perceived every party was on a different subject. . . . A cluster of wives I observed were calling for a bible to decide a dispute they had enter'd into, whether minced-Pyes or Plumb Porridge, were the properest Food on Christmas day. A devout old lady argued against Plumb porridge. She was answered with warmth by a couple of ladies thirty years younger than herself . . . A call to the Tea table put a stop to this delightful controversy. They went into one room to their tea and we men into another room to our bottle, over which I was entertained to a tedious repetition of the elections of common council-men and who I thought would carry it for chamberlain &c. &c.

After the commonwealth London extended herself slowly but surely. If we are to believe contemporary writers it was not altogether a beautiful extension. The scenes which Ned Ward depicts in his famous *London Spy* of 1699 are perhaps the black and grey spots of London, but they bear the stamp of truth, and I will quote some specimens taken from an excellent summary in the *Gentleman's Magazine* of 1857, as they will explain better than anything else this aspect of seventeenth century London.

At the outset of the work we have a description of a common coffee-house of the day, one of the many hundreds with which London then teemed Although coffee had been known in England only some fifty years, coffee-houses were already among the most favourite institutions of the land —

'Come,' says my friend, 'let us step into this coffee-house here; as you are a stranger in the town, it will afford you some diversion.' Accordingly in we went, where a parcel of muddling muckworms were as busy as so many rats in an old cheese-loft; some going, some coming, some scribbling some talking, some drinking, some smoking, others jangling; and the whole room stinking of tobacco, like a Dutch scoot, [schuyt,] or a boatswain's cabin. The walls were hung round with gilt frames, as a farrier's shop with horse-shoes, which contained abundance of rarities, viz Nectar and Ambrosia, May-dew, Golden Elixirs, Popular Pills, Liquid Snuff, Beautifying Waters, Dentifrices, Drops, and Lozenges; all as infallible as the Pope, 'Where every one (as the famous Saffold has it) above the rest, Deservedly has gain'd the name of best' every medicine being so catholic, it pretends to nothing less than universality. So that, had not my friend told me 'twas a coffee-house, I should have taken it for Quacks' Hall, or the parlour of some eminent mountebank. We each of us stuck in our mouths a pipe of sotweed, and now began to look about us.

In the course of a few pages we have another description of London :—

The modest hour of nine was now proclaimed by time's oracle from every steeple; and the joyful alarm of Bow-bell called the weary apprentices from their work to their paring-shovels, to unhitch their folded shutters, and button up their shops till the next morning. The streets were all adorned with dazzling lights,

whose bright reflect so glittered in my eyes, that I
could see nothing but themselves. Thus I walked
amazed, like a wandering soul in its pilgrimage to
heaven, when he passes through the spangled regions.
My ears were serenaded on every side, with the grave
music of sundry passing-bells, the rattling of coaches,
and the melancholy ditties of hot bak'd wardens and
pippins.

Two hours later the scene is vastly changed —

Each parochial Jack of Lanthorn was now croaking
about streets the hour of eleven. The brawny topers
of the city began now to forsake the tavern, and
stagger, haulking after a poop-lanthorn, to their own
homes. Augusta appeared in her mourning weeds;
and the glittering lamps which a few hours before
sparkled like diamonds fix'd as ornaments to her sable
dress, were now dwindled to a glimmering snuff, and
burnt as dim as torches at a prince's funeral.

The night's adventures are concluded by a lodging
in sorry plight at the Dark House, in Billingsgate, the
company, furniture, and discomforts of which are
humorously but coarsely described. Quitting their
pigstye in the morning (for little better does the
' Dark House ' seem to have been), they visit the
Monument and Gresham College, the museum of which
last affords Ned a rare opportunity of exercising his
wit. After taking a peep at Bedlam—one of the grand
peep-shows, by the way, of the day—our friends arrive
at the Royal Exchange, the predecessor of the present
structure. It was built by Edward Jerman, the city
surveyor, to supply the place of Gresham's building,
which had been destroyed in the Fire of London.
The scene presented by the exterior is first described —

The .... cum

were adorned with sundry memorandums of old age
and infirmity, under which stood here and there a
Jack in a Box, selling cures for your corns, glass eyes
for the blind, ivory teeth for broken mouths, and spec-
tacles for the weak-sighted; the passage to the gate
being lined with hawkers, gardeners, mandrake-sellers,
and porters.   After we crowded a little way amongst
this miscellaneous multitude, we came to a pippin-
monger's stall, surmounted with a chemist's shop:
where Drops, Elixirs, Cordials, and Balsams had justly
the pre-eminence of apples, chestnuts pears, and oranges;
the former being ranked in as much order upon shelves
as the works of the holy fathers in a bishop's library,
and the latter being marshall'd with as much exactness
as an army ready to engage.   Here is drawn up several
regiments of Kentish pippins, next some squadrons of
pearmains, join'd to a brigade of small-nuts, with a
few troops of booncritons, all form'd into a battalion,
the wings composed of oranges lemons, pomegranates,
dried plums, and medlars.

They then venture a step further, and 'go on to the
'Change'.   In the interior—

Advertisements hung as thick round the pillars of
each walk as bells about the legs of a morris-dancer,
and an incessant buz, like the murmurs of the distant
ocean, stood as a diapason to our talk, like a drone to
a bagpipe.   The wainscot was adorned with quacks'
bills, instead of pictures; never an empiric in the town
but had his name in a lacquered frame, containing an
invitation for a fool and his money to be soon parted;
and he that wants a dry rogue for himself, or a wet-
nurse for a child, may be furnished here at a minute's
warning

Leaving the walk below, they ascend to what was
then known as the ' Pawn '; galleries fitted up for the
sale of fancy goods, gloves, ribbons, ruffles, bands, &c.,

not unlike the stalls in the bazaars of the present day :—

Accordingly we went up, where women sat in their pinfolds, begging of custom, with such amorous looks and affable tones, that I could not but fancy they had as much mind to dispose of themselves as the commodities they deal in. My ears on both sides were so baited with 'Fine linen, Sir,' and 'Gloves and ribbons, Sir,' that I had a milliner's and a sempstress's shop in my head for a week after.

St. Paul's was at this period within some ten years of its completion. The author's somewhat disjointed and fragmentary description extends over several pages of the book, from which the following may be gathered.—

From thence we turned through the west gate of St. Paul's Churchyard; where we saw a parcel of stone-cutters and sawyers, so very hard at work that I protest, notwithstanding the vehemency of their labour, and the temperateness of the season, instead of using their handkerchiefs to wipe the sweat off their faces, they were most of them blowing their nails. We thence moved up a long wooden bridge, that led to the west porticum of the church, where we intermixed with such a promiscuous rabble that I fancied we looked like the beasts driving into the ark, to replenish a succeeding world. From thence we entered the body of the church, the spaciousness of which we could not discern for the largeness of the pillars. We now went a little further, where we observed ten men in a corner, very busy about two men's work. The wonderful piece of difficulty the whole number had to perform was to drag along a stone of about three hundredweight, in a carriage, in order to be hoisted upon the mouldings of the cupola; but they were so long in hauling on't half the length of the church, that a couple of lusty porters in the same time would have carried it to Paddington without resting of their burthen. From thence we approached the quire on the north side the entrance of which had been very much defaced by the late fire, occasioned by the carelessness of a plumber, who had been mending some defective pipes of the organ ; which unhappy accident has given the dissenters so far an opportunity to reflect upon the use of music in our churches, that they scruple not to vent their spleen by saying, ''Twas a judgment from heaven upon their carvings and their fopperies, for displeasing the ears of the Almighty with the profane tootings of such abominable cat-calls.' When prayers were over, we returned into the body of the church, happily intermixed with a crowd of good Christians, who had concluded with us their afternoon's devotion. We now took notice of the vast distance of the pillars, from whence they turn the cupola , on which, they say, is a spire to be erected three hundred feet in height, whose towering pinnacle will stand with such stupenduous loftiness above Bow-steeple dragon, or the Monument's flaming urn, that it will appear to the rest of the holy temples like a cedar of Lebanon among so many shrubs, or a Goliath looking over the shoulders of so many Davids.

After passing through Smithfield Rounds, ' which entertained his nostrils with such a savoury scent of roast meat, and surprised his ears with the jingling noise of so many jacks, that he stared about him like a country bumpkin in Spittlefields, among so many throwster's mills,' Ned and his friend make their way to the rails —

Where country carters stood armed with their long whips, to keep their teams upon sale in a due decorum, who were drawn up into the most sightly order with their forefeet mounted on a dunghill, and their heads dressed up to as much advantage as an Inns-of-court

sempstress, or the mistress of a boarding-school ; some
with their manes frizzled up, to make 'em appear
high-withered ; others with their manes plaited, as if
they had been ridden by the night-mare : and the
fellows that attended them making as uncouth figures
as the monsters in the *Tempest*. We then went a little
further, and there we saw a parcel of ragged rapscallions,
mounted upon scrubbed [scrub] tits, scouring about the
Rounds, some trotting, some galloping, some pacing,
and others stumbling : blundering about in that con-
fusion, that I thought them like so many beggars on
horseback, riding to the devil.

Returning through the Lame Hospital now better
known as Bartholomew's, and passing through Christ's
Hospital, '*alias* the Blew-Coat School, where abundance
of little children, in blue jackets and kite-lanthorn'd
caps, were very busy at their several recreations,' Ned
and his friend move on till they arrive at Fleet
Bridge :—

Where nuts gingerbread, oranges, and oysters lay
pil'd up in moveable shops, that run upon wheels,
attended by ill-looking fellows, some with but one eye
and others without noses. Over against these stood
a parcel of trugmoldies, in straw-hats and flat-caps,
selling socks and furmity, night-caps and plum-
pudding

This bridge connected Ludgate Hill with Fleet Street,
and was finally removed in 1765, the period at which
Fleet Ditch was arched over and hidden from view.

An interesting relic of this period is the room of
No. 17, Fleet Street (see p. 181), with its beautiful
ceiling and panelling. It was probably the Council
Room of Prince Henry of Wales, built about 1610–11
for the official quarters of the Duchy of Lancaster and
purchased by the County Council in 1900.

Whatever results we may draw from these notes, one thing is certain—that London has lost its control over its own destinies   Citizenship with these surroundings was a different kind of citizenship from the old burghal citizenship of previous days.   Interests were divergent and distracting, control did not extend beyond very narrow limits.   The London which gambled with its life in the fashion of the Tudors and Stuarts was not the ordered municipal city of the Plantagenets.

One aspect of London life must be considered before passing to our final story.   The influence of the river in the evolution of London having been noted, it will be well to indicate its position in late historical times. Whenever any one desired to proceed from one end of the city to the other, the means which he would adopt as being both the most convenient and the most pleasant would be by boat on the river.   Even more would this be the case when proceeding beyond the city to such places on the river-side as Greenwich, Fulham, &c. Communication between London and the outlying districts by road was tedious, disagreeable, and accompanied by risk.   The roads were such as would hardly deserve the name at the present day, in bad weather almost impassable, and haunted by the footpad and highwayman.   Coaches did not come into use much before the seventeenth century, and even then were expensive and badly hung. which circumstance, with the bad condition of the roads, made a journey in them not an agreeable experience.   So it was again that the most speedy, the safest, and by far the most pleasant means of conveyance was by river.   Indeed, the recognized route from London to the west was by river as far

as Putney, and thence by road over Putney Heath
This was the course naturally adopted by Wolsey,
when, having been deprived of the Great Seal, he was
retiring in disgrace to his seat at Esher. He had
come by water from York House (Whitehall) to
Putney, and was proceeding up Putney Hill when he
was overtaken by the messenger who had been dis-
patched to assure him of the continuance of the Royal
favour.

From no source do we get a more graphic picture of
the river as a highway than from the pages of Pepys'
Diary. 'By water to White Hall,' 'So by water home,'
'By water to the Temple,' 'Down by water to Dept-
ford,' are phrases continually recurring in his accounts
of his everyday official life. But the river also occupied an important place in his pleasure excursions.
He goes to the bear gardens on the opposite bank, or
takes his wife to Vauxhall. On several occasions he
ascends the river as far as Barn Elms. 'After dinner by
water, the day being mighty pleasant, and the tide
serving finely, reading in Boyle's book of colours, as
high as Barne Elmes, and there took one turn alone,
and then back to Putney church, where I saw the
girls of the schools, few of which pretty' (28th April,
1667). Sometimes he took Mrs. Pepys with him on
these excursions. 'I and my wife and Mercer up by
water to Barne Elmes, where we walked by moonshine,
and called at Lambeth and drank and had cold meat
in the boat, and did eat and sing, and down home by
almost twelve at night, very fine and pleasant, only
could not sing ordinary songs with the freedom that
otherwise I would' (21st July, 1667).

Every facility existed for persons desiring to take

boat. The landing-places along the river-bank, 'stairs' they were called, were very numerous: in 1707 there were over a hundred. To meet the demands of the public, many hundreds of watermen found constant employment on the river. From Taylor, the water poet we learn that in the reign of Elizabeth 'the number of watermen, and those that live and are maintained by them, and by the onely labour of the oare and the scull, betwixt the bridge of Windsor and Gravesend, cannot be fewer than forty thousand'.[1] The number seems to have been the same in the reign of Anne, for Strype says: 'There be 40,000 watermen upon the rolls of the Company [Watermen's Company] as I have been told by one of the Company: and that upon occasion they can furnish 20000 men for the fleet; and that there were 8,000 then in the service.'[2] These numbers have now much decreased owing to the comparative disuse of the river. This has been brought about partly by the construction of bridges and tunnels, affording other means of crossing the river, and partly by the facilities offered by cab, omnibus, tramcar, and railway, which have to a great extent drawn passenger traffic away from the river; and by steamboats, which, while retaining the use of the river, have nevertheless completely changed the whole character of the passenger traffic thereon.

It will thus be seen that in these times the river must have presented a constant scene of life and activity. Touches of brilliancy, moreover, were never wanting. Here and there on the river-bank were the palaces of royalty and the mansions of nobility, each

[1] *The True Cause of the Watermen's Suit concerning Players, &c*, p 172
[2] Strype's *Stow* book v p 232

provided with its access to the river In Tudor times, for instance, there were royal residences at Greenwich, The Tower, Bridewell, Whitehall, Westminster, Chelsea, and further up the river as far as Windsor, and it was a common sight to see the magnificent royal barges or the splendid barges of the nobility, manned by their bargemen in gorgeous liveries and badges, sweeping up and down the river. In addition, the corporation of the city of London and the great city companies had their barges and liveried attendants.

At a time when the river was the great highway of London it was natural that great pageants and ceremonies should often be held on the water. For centuries the Lord Mayor's show proceeded to Westminster by water, and it was not until 1857 that, the rights of the City of London corporation as conservators of the Thames then lapsing, the journey was performed by land On a new ambassador coming to the country it was the custom for him to travel by land as far as Gravesend, where he was met by the Lord Mayor and aldermen, and conducted in state by river to the Tower Stairs, whence he proceeded by state coach to Whitehall

The public entry into London of Catherine of Braganza, consort of Charles II, must have been one of the most gorgeous pageants ever witnessed from the Thames banks. She came from Hampton Court to Whitehall, and Evelyn mentions 'the innumerable boats and vessels, dressed and adorned with all imaginable pomp, but, above all, the thrones, arches, pageants, and other representations, stately barges of the Lord Mayor and Companies, with various inventions, music, and peals of ordnance'

The Thames has changed again since those days and pleasure and picturesque pageantry have deserted it, though a pageantry of another kind has arisen. It was the centre of Tudor and Stuart life in London as it was of earlier times right through the centuries. If Tudor and Stuart life was less homogeneous, less of a city life and more of a town life, it is the link which connects the city of London in the fullness of its communal existence with the county of London struggling to obtain a recognized place for London among the capital cities of the world.

CHAPTER XX

LONDON AS THE EMPIRE CITY

THE nineteenth century witnessed the growth of
a very great London, great in extent, in population,
in wealth, but not a city with its own special ideals
apart from the ideals it has inherited I believe these
will come as soon as Englishmen have learned the
lesson, known to the citizens of antiquity, that city life
is the true method of civilization. We have seen in
the past how difficult it has been for the Englishman
to learn this truth. It has not come completely home
to him yet. and the ideals of London have not come
yet. All we have to do then is to try to comprehend
the London which has evolved from all those positions
in the past which we have been considering.

The growth began, as we have seen, in Tudor times.
It spread along the Strand, on the river side of which
were built mansions of the nobility, with gardens
extending to the water's edge. Essex House, Arundel
House, Somerset House, the Palace of the Savoy.
Worcester House Salisbury House, Durham House,
York House, and Northumberland House are amongst
the most familiar examples leaving to us street names
to tell of former conditions. It extended from Southwark, also along the banks of the river. The next
extension. just after the Fire. is north of the city area

towards Old Street. Three-quarters of a century later
(1745) we get a great extension all round up to Hyde
Park on the west, just north of Oxford Street, Theo-
bald's Road, and Old Street on the north, to White-
chapel and Limehouse on the east. Another fifty
years (1799) we have a further fringe of narrow
dimensions penetrating to Knightsbridge on the west,
creeping up to Edgware Road, taking in the southern
part of Marylebone, extending to Camden Town, adding
to the 1745 extension in the east a narrow belt all
round, and finally showing the first great extension in
north Lambeth along the banks of the river. In 1832
the Regent's Park district on the north, a large district
of Lambeth on the south, and a further extension of
Bermondsey and Southwark are the principal features.
Islington, St. Pancras, Shoreditch, Bethnal Green, and
Mile End also filled up at this date, together with
a little bit of Greenwich. In 1862 the great era of
building set in, and all round the boundary of the 1832
limits we have great extensions The next stage is
1887, which again shows an extension of the building
area all round the map; and now, twenty-four years
later, we have scarcely any boundary of London left,
for building has gone on spreading into Kent, Surrey,
Middlesex, and Essex at a pace which almost defies
exact description

The city proper is the centre of the business world
of London. It contains the Bank of England, the
head offices of the great banking and insurance companies, and the offices and warehouses of the principal
merchants The city churches, nearly one hundred in
number, are conspicuous features, while the great
cathedral of St. Paul's, Wren's masterpiece, dominates

the city as the principal feature from whatever point
the city is seen.

The county completely surrounds the city, extending
from Bow on the east to Hammersmith on the west,
from Hampstead on the north to Tooting on the south,
and taking in Hackney on the north-east, Woolwich
on the south-east, and extending to Putney on the
south-west. It contains more of London life than the
city proper. That it is the seat of Imperial Government has already been noted, and the significance
historically has been worked out. The Houses of
Parliament and the whole of the Government offices
and the Law Courts are the material representatives
of this unique position. The Mint, Trinity House, the
Inns of Court, the Tower of London, the cathedral
church of Southwark, the Abbey Church of Westminster, the Roman Catholic cathedral church, the
arsenal of Woolwich, the King's Palace, the town residence of the Prince of Wales, the town houses of
the nobility and aristocracy, and the palaces of the
Archbishop of Canterbury and the Bishop of London
are all in the county. It is the seat of two bishoprics,
namely, London and Southwark. It contains Eltham
Palace, one of the favourite residences of the kings of
England, particularly of Henry VIII and including
Charles I. Greenwich Palace, which Henry VIII,
Queen Mary, and Queen Elizabeth occupied : Kensington Palace, where William III, Mary II, Anne, and
George II died, and Queen Victoria was born : and
many beautiful buildings of historic importance Most
of the principal railway terminus stations are in the
county It has also very large manufacturing and
industrial centres which make London the largest

manufacturing city in the world. It is the centre of all institutions for amusements, the Albert Hall, and all the theatres, music halls, hotels, &c. The University of London and its schools and colleges are also situated in the county, as are the British Museum, the Natural History Museum, South Kensington Museum, the National Gallery, the National Portrait Gallery, the Tate Gallery, the Wallace Collection, and other galleries and museums. It is the seat also of all the principal learned societies, located chiefly at Burlington House, and Greenwich Observatory, upon which practically the time of the world is based, is within the county area of London.

The story of the expansion is mainly topographical. Its meaning and effect is one of the problems of political institutions The strangest thing is that with a city such as London, capital of an empire such as the British, there should be so little real recognition of its position. Londoners do not recognize it; Parliament does not recognize it, statesmen do not recognize it—do not recognize it, I mean, in a definite, comprehensive way, as Paris or Berlin is recognized, do not take it to themselves as one of the institutions of the country with definite relationship to other institutions. It is not so recognized in politics, in sentiment, or in literature There is only a sort of hushed acknowledgement of it. Visitors come up to London, but Londoners receive them in Kensington, Paddington, Dulwich, Poplar, St. Pancras, or other local centre. London is not London to the vast majority of Londoners, but a place.

The empire city is there, however, in the full strength of its position. It is the centre of govern-

ment, of commerce and industry, of shipping, of
learning, of enterprise, of progress.   If it is governed
with no sense of unity, the unity is springing up in
spite of obstacles   If its history is what I have endeavoured to sketch out, the effect of that history is
going to work its way into the minds of future
generations.   It is impossible for such a history to be
absolutely sterilized.   Fragments of it are talked about
and extolled.   People are beginning to care about the
houses in which great men and women have lived or
died, and note with interest the placques which an
enlightened governing authority affix to record the
facts.   Scholars and artists are still interested in what
London has to tell them   The atmosphere of London
is all-embracing.   And when once it is understood
how great the story of it is, how London alone of all
British cities is the capital city without a rival for its
place—is capital city not because of formal appoint-
ment thereto, but because of the great position it has
occupied in the country for nearly nineteen centuries,
as Roman city, as city-state, as municipal city, as
national city, as empire city; then its sons and
daughters will see to it that they, in their pride of
it, will give all the tribute that is due.

The name of London is now properly and legally
applied to two well-defined areas: the ancient city
with which we have had so much to do in these pages,
and the county constituted by Act of Parliament in
1888.   And I will point out here the interesting
analogy which this has to the much earlier condition
of things when there were two Londons, Boudicca's
London, as we may term it, and Lundinium Augusta.
I have noted the indications of the preservation of the

smaller London surrounded by the greater Augusta,
and I have noted that the name of London, preserved
to us by the inner area, finally triumphed over that of
Augusta, and was applied eventually to the whole
city with its walls, its pomerium, and its territorium.
The two Londons of to-day are precisely in the same
position. Ancient London, protected by the sentiment
and affection of its citizens, remains intact. Modern
London, surrounding it and enclosing it, absorbing
it in certain directions, takes the name of London for
its whole area. We thus have repeated in the nineteenth century of London's history what was enacted
in the first century, and it is not a little remarkable
that so true an analogy can be drawn.

The government of this dual area, of these two Londons, is not even dual. It is multiple. It is the direct
product of the singular neglect of the London growing
up around the city which, as we have seen, aroused the
jealousy and alarm of the Stuart monarchs and statesmen. No government of any comprehensive kind was
given to this area until 1855. Prior to that date there
were the Justices of the Peace for Middlesex, Surrey,
and Kent exercising jurisdiction in the parts belonging
to those counties, and there were commissioners appointed by the Crown to deal with main drainage,
highway boards to deal with roads, and officers to deal
with buildings For the rest there was nothing but
the ancient parish constitution and even the manorial
institution to rely upon, upon which were intruded
all sorts of paving and other boards by a series of Acts
of Parliament as curious as they are disgraceful. The
chaos was ridiculous. Thus, as an example, let me note
the different paving boards which existed to govern the

Strand from No. 1 to Temple Bar. They came in the following order. (1) St. Martin's alone; (2) St. Martin's and St Clement's; (3) St. Martin's and the Savoy; (4) Savoy and St. Clement's; (5) Savoy and St. Mary's; (6) St. Mary's alone; (7) St. Mary's and Somerset Place; (8) St. Mary's alone; (9) St Clement's alone— the distance being 1,336 yards or three-quarters of a mile, and there being nine divisions. Cecil Street, a street running from the Strand towards the river, with a carriage-way about ten yards wide, was under two separate managements, namely, St Martin's and St Clement's. Along Wellington Street North, from the north end of Exeter Street to the south side of the Strand, a distance of 100 yards, there were four separate jurisdictions, namely, St. Paul's, Covent Garden, St Martin's St. Clement's, and Savoy. Altogether the number of different local Acts in force in London prior to 1855 was about 250, independent of public general acts, administered by not less than 300 different bodies; 137 of these returned members numbering no less than 4,738 persons. For the other boards there were 5,710 more members, so that the whole area was governed by no less than 10,448 persons.

But this is not all. There is a remarkable series of Acts of Parliament for building on the great estates comprised in the London area. We owe great and lasting benefits to these Acts in the beautiful system of laying out on a town-planning system much of the central part of London. There are no less than 365 squares in London, many of them of singular charm and beauty. But the methods adopted for administering these squares are simply amazing. I will quote

only one example, that of the Southampton Estate
Act of 1801 (41 Geo. III, cap. 131). By this Act 'the
owner, or owners, of the freehold and inheritance, his,
her, and their heirs and assigns', together with certain
persons named in the Act (the lessees), are 'appointed
commissioners for carrying this Act into execution',
and it is imposed upon the commissioners ' to cause
the several streets, squares, and other public passages
and places to be made and set out within the limits of
this Act to be paved'; also 'to be cleansed, lighted,
watched, and watered' (sect. 13); 'to cause such lamp-
irons and lamp-posts to be put up or fixed upon or
against the walls or pallisadoes of any of the houses,
tenements, or buildings and inclosures, or in such other
manner within the said intended streets, squares, or other
public passages and places as they shall think proper';
'to cause to be painted, engraved, or described . . . the
name by which each respective street, square, lane, &c..
is to be properly called or known', 'to cause all or any
of the streets, squares, &c., to be watered,' for which
purpose they may 'cause such number of wells and
pumps to be dug, sunk, and made as they shall think
necessary' (sect 18), and, finally, 'to appoint such
number of watchmen and patroles' as they shall think
proper, providing 'them with proper arms, ammuni-
tion, weapons, and cloathing for the discharge of their
duty.' In return for these services the commissioners
are empowered to levy 'one or more rate or rates,
assessment or assessments, . . . upon all houses, shops,
warehouses, coach-houses, stables, cellars, vaults, buildings, and tenements in any of the said streets, squares.
&c.' (sect. 37).

I do not think it is necessary to go further than

this. Not only administrative duties of the widest
kind but police duties with armed police were
entrusted to these self-constituted commissioners.
Every reader will understand the magnitude of the
interests which had been established in London by
this remarkable legislation. There is nothing like it
in the United Kingdom. It is scarcely believable of
London except that London has been for so long the
sporting ground of legislative experiments—not experiments on a large scale to try what institutions could
do if properly endowed with powers and duties, but
experiments on a singularly petty scale, bred as it
seems to me of a universal mistrust of what London
might become if she were allowed to develop naturally
as she developed in the early days and proved herself
capable of taking a great part in great events.

The Act of 1855 constituting a special form of
government for what was called the Metropolis was
a signal failure. It conformed to no possible ideal of
English local self-government, and it fell by its own
weakness The Act of 1888, restoring popular government to the counties of England after a lapse of some
seven hundred years, also gave to London its first real
chance of self-government. Chaos still reigns, unfor-
tunately. One could not expect simplicity to follow
the astounding chaos of past ages. But simplicity is
growing more and more to be the ideal of statesman-
ship, municipal and Parliamentary, and some day it
will reveal itself in London.

It is not my purpose now to proceed further in this
direction The making of London has been traced out
from earliest beginnings in the Roman empire to
present position in the British empire The greatness

of her activities in all branches of human affairs does
not enter into our subject, and details are easily avail-
able to students who want to understand London from
other aspects. I have been concerned with the making
of London as an example of the evolution of a great
city. It has not been possible to tell the whole story,
but I have told the essentials. It is a story of great
beginnings, great mishaps, great struggles, but withal
a glorious story. It is the living history of an institution—a history that is not only generally unknown
but is often denied by writers of eminence and knowledge. The neglect of such a history is shameful.
London has as much right to pay due respect to
its ancient traditions, to its continuous customs, to its
archaeological remains, to its constitutional and legal
rights and powers, as ever Paris or Rome or Athens
had or has. Scholars are ready to attribute value of
an important degree to the chance preservation of
minute relics relating to these and other places
of antiquity. The making of London is not recorded
in minute relics. They are great and manifest. But
they have not only to be dug up out of records or
from beneath the ground; they have to be insisted
upon. A Roman remain in London tells the same story
as in any other city. If there are no Anglo-Saxon
monuments inside the city it is because they were
placed outside the city—at Thorney Island, at Kingston,
in the fields, in the planning of our parishes and manors,
even in the alignment of our streets. If Norman
monuments still exist to tell us of the strength of this
new element of London they are only typical of what
Norman London actually became. If Plantagenet
remains are scattered and few and very beautiful, they

depict the gradually forming city of the nation.   If
Tudor and Stuart relics bring us straight on to modern
London, telling us of an uncontrollable development, as
careless as the times and the thought which belonged
to the times, we are prepared for that chaos in government which the early nineteenth century witnessed.
There is continuity in this story, unbroken continuity,
and gazing back across the centuries Londoners must
learn that in the history of their own city there is contained so much that is worth knowing not only on its
own account but also on account of its importance in the
history of the nation. A nation cannot have such a city
as London, possessed of such a history, without being
profoundly influenced by it. Everyone who has followed
the situation as it has been unfolded in these pages
must appreciate the enormous and continuous influence
of London in the shaping of the nation   That influence
has been uniformly good.   There have been few, very
few, mad moments, and there have been innumerable
great moments.   The nation owes much to London, and
the story of the evolution of the city is the record of
that debt.

There is scarcely a foot of ground in London that is
not consecrated to her history.   Milton's house was
in Aldersgate, Dryden's in Fetter Lane, Crosby Hall
enclosed a spot on which William Shakespeare undoubtedly stood, Christ's Hospital was a London
foundation of great importance, Sir Paul Pinder's
house in Bishopsgate was a typical citizen's house,
Drury Lane was originally the home of the opulent
citizen who preferred to live outside the city in Stuart
days—and all have disappeared.   In the midst of this
destruction, often senseless destruction, it is interesting

to find the element of preservation getting stronger. The Government in 1909 stopped the destruction of Chelsea Hospital; the County Council in 1911 has preserved by purchase the beautiful almshouses in the Kingsland Road, erected by the Ironmongers' company in 1715 and representing a good example of Mid-Georgian architecture.

And now my task is done. 'The Thames has made London' are the words with which I began, and if any one wishes to test that proposition let him take his stand at the end of the pier at Southend—vulgar, cockney, beautiful Southend—on a bright spring morning, in the haze of the early summer, with the coming winter thick upon him, in the midst of winter snows, sleets, and winds—let him take his stand there and watch the pageant of ships steaming along from all ends of the world to their destiny in London The same scene on a limited scale was seen by ancestors of his in the first century, and in the eleventh century where the first definite record has been noted. The world was not so extensive in those far-off periods, but it was the whole world of commerce then, as it is the whole world of commerce now. During the long intervening years, of which these are but the signal posts, the same thing has gone on. The river has deepened its course, the shallows have largely disappeared, the shores have changed, but the river Thames stands to London for what it has always stood, and London stands to the nation and the empire as the greatest city the world has ever seen.

INDEX

OXFORD   HORACE HART, M A
PRINTER TO THE UNIVERSITY

Lightning Source UK Ltd.
Milton Keynes UK
UKHW020627260722
406393UK00005B/778